A Pocket Guide to Sects and New Religions

Nigel Scotland

LION

A Lion Book
an imprint of
Lion Hudson plc
Mayfield House, 256 Banbury Road,
Oxford OX2 7DH, England
www.lionhudson.com
ISBN 0 7459 5159 7

First edition 2005
10 9 8 7 6 5 4 3 2 1 0

Text Acknowledgments
pp. 30, 32, 36, 75, 87, 106, 107, 228 Scripture quotations
taken from the Holy Bible, New International Version,
copyright © 1973, 1978, 1984 International Bible Society.
Used by permission of Zondervan and Hodder &
Stoughton Limited. All rights reserved. The 'NIV' and
'New International Version' trademarks are registered
in the United States Patent and Trademark Office by
International Bible Society. Use of either trademark
requires the permission of International Bible Society.
UK trademark number 1448790.

A catalogue record for this book is available
from the British Library

Typeset in 10/13 Palatino Medium
Printed and bound in Malta

Contents

Preface

One of the striking features at the beginning of the third millennium is the growing array of new religions on offer. In the last three decades there has been an upsurge in the number of religious groups actively and publicly seeking a following. That said, the phenomenon of religion is as old as the human race itself. The word 'religion', which is frequently understood to mean traditions that are passed down, is not easy to define in precise terms. The Romans used the Latin word *religio* to refer to rituals they performed in honour of the gods. Cicero (c. 106–43 BCE) used 'religio' in this way in his book *On the Nature of the Gods*. There is also a sense in which such rituals bind people together in terms of beliefs, practices and values and this in turn produces a coherent world view and way of life. Most scholars are agreed that its central focus involves a group or groups of people reverencing or propitiating some form of deity and establishing in consequence a particular lifestyle and code of behaviour. The majority of religions considered in this *Pocket Guide* are in this category.

Most religions have a core of common characteristics. They have scriptures or holy books, essential beliefs and sacred meetings where there is prayer, chanting or meditation. In many cases these meetings necessitate special furniture and artefacts.

Religious institutions all urge particular codes of behaviour on their followers that are felt to be beneficial to them as well as pleasing to the deities. Experience of one kind or another lies at the heart of most religions. This is frequently both inward and external. It is inward in the sense that feelings such as peace, calm, tranquillity, wholeness or increased self-awareness are conveyed. It is external in that members share with others in various rituals which have the effect of creating deep bonds and emotional attachments.

All religious institutions both impact, and in turn, are impacted by the society of which they are a part. This interaction inevitably has a political and social dimension as devotees may reject values, cultures and sometimes national legislation. Christadelphians and Jehovah's Witnesses, for example, are pacifist and refuse to take part in occupations connected with the military. Conversely, the values of surrounding cultures often rub off on core religious beliefs and values. This might account for groups such as The Branch Davidians, Osho International and The Family engaging in libertine sexual relationships after having begun with traditional values. The recent and growing popularity of female deities may be viewed as arising, in part at least, from the emergence of feminism since the 1960s and particularly in the last decade of the twentieth century.

Religious movements often have strong political agendas, as was witnessed in George W. Bush's election in 2004 to serve a second term as president of the United States, carried to power by the votes of the conservative evangelical Christian groups of Middle America in particular. In terms of new religions, Aum Shinrikyô sought to gain a hearing for its beliefs by setting up its own political organization, The Supreme Truth Party, and fielding candidates for the Japanese House of Representatives. The

Transcendental Meditation movement established The Natural Law Party with the specific aim of influencing the policies of national governments. A number of groups considered in this book have great reverence for the earth, which they hold to be divine or at the very least a conscious living being. This has led some to develop strong political agendas and make fierce defences of the earth's resources, sometimes in direct opposition to government policies.

Two major factors have impacted religion in the Western world in recent decades; the growing multicultural nature of society and the emergence of scepticism and doubt in the wake of modernity and postmodernity. The presence in the West of significant numbers of peoples from the Asian subcontinent and from the developing nations has brought a wide range of Muslim, Hindu and Buddhist spiritualities to the doorstep of Western homes. Growing awareness of these traditions has been further increased by cheap air travel and developments in electronic communication. For many who have become disenchanted with the dull, cerebral aridity of Western Christianity these Eastern traditions offer practical holistic therapies and experiential immediacy with the promise of self-realization and fulfilment. Additionally, the growing clamour of voices resulting from this religious pluralism in the West has meant that those who seek a hearing for their new teachings can feel themselves compelled to use intensive methods of persuasion on those who attend their worship gatherings and enquiry courses. In some cases this has led to accusation of people's freedoms being curtailed or restricted.

This *Pocket Guide* considers the world's most popular new religions. Most have their roots either in one of the major world faiths or in recent culture. Some, such as the Christadelphians,

Jehovah's Witnesses, Christian Science and Oneness Pentecostalism, have their roots in historic Christianity. The Bahá'ís, the Nation of Islam and the Sufi Order of the West are among those who draw on Islamic practice and doctrine. Groups such as Elan Vital, the Brahma Kumaris, the Satya Sai Baba Society and ISKCON have emerged out of Hindu traditions. Others, such as the Spiritualists, Freemasons, Rosicrucianism and Theosophy, have their roots in esoteric philosophical thought, while some more recent organizations such as Heaven's Gate, the Church of Scientology and the Raëlians have been largely influenced by contemporary culture. In all cases the basic information regarding origins, belief and practice set out in the following chapters has been derived from the movements' own resources, books, magazines and other literature. In some instances the information has been read and commented on by members themselves.

The book sets out to offer an objective account of each religion providing details of their origins, core beliefs, recent developments and present day practice. Although the title is *Sects & New Religions*, neither term need be regarded as pejorative. The term 'sect' has a fairly long history and was first developed by the German sociologist Ernst Troeltsch (1865–1923) to denote small, vibrant groups who separated themselves from the larger national churches that had emerged in the centuries following the European Reformation. Sects, like most religious groups, may be said to have their good and bad moments. However, many have a solid track record when it comes to upholding orthodox teachings and moral standards. Many are also very caring and practically supportive of their members. Where there is worship, it is often vibrant and participatory, which gives members a sense of belonging and personal worth.

On the other hand, sects are often led by a strong, sometimes over-dominant leader; they tend to read their sacred texts with literalness and often have an inflated sense of a conflict between good and evil. Along with almost all new religions included in this volume, they believe that theirs is the one living and unchanging truth. Many of the major sects and those that are most popular in the contemporary world emerged before 1900.

'New religion' within the context of this Pocket Guide refers primarily to movements that have emerged since the 1970s. Many are led by individuals who declare themselves to be a messiah figure or are subsequently accorded divine status by their followers. They frequently operate very strict regimes that include high levels of personal commitment and involve intensive religious exercises. In some instances the core members are secluded from their surrounding society and live in communes or reservations. Indeed some leave the world outside altogether, believing it to be doomed to destruction. Some have sought to purge it by destroying its inhabitants or to escape from it by committing suicide, as in the case of Heaven's Gate.

Not all the religious institutions considered in this book fit precisely into these two categories. Some such as Wicca, Druidism, Freemasonry and the Theosophical Movement are probably best regarded as alternative spiritualities. The focus of these is the self rather than any particular deity. The goal is to tap into the divine spark within or in some cases discover god within. Alternative spiritualities often seek to achieve this awareness by means of prescribed religious exercises such as chanting mantras or engaging in New Age holistic and natural therapies. Unlike the members of sects and new religious movements, those who engage in alternative spiritualities tend not to draw rigid lines of demarcation between themselves and others.

On a concluding note, it is important to bear in mind that no religion remains the same for long. There is a constant updating of beliefs and practices. Religious institutions such as the Children of God (now known as The Family) and the Unification Church, to name but two, have changed considerably in recent years, the former rejecting its extreme libertine sexuality, the latter becoming much more open in its attitudes to other religious organizations. Equally, some of those who were a part of the radical Jesus Movement of the 1970s have since become solid establishment figures. New and contemporary religion must therefore be appraised cautiously in the light of its current state, not on the basis of rigid and stereotypical judgments.

1. Aum Shinrikyô

Origins

Chizuo Matsumoto (b. 1955), a former acupuncturist and yoga instructor who later took the name Shoko Asahara, founded Aum Shinsen no Kai in 1986. He moved to Tokyo in 1977 and studied acupuncture and traditional Chinese medicine. He married the following year and he and his wife sold herbal medicines. At this time Asahara developed an intense religion and committed himself to Agonshu, a new religious movement that taught freedom from bad karma through good deeds and meditation. At a later stage, when Asahara formed his own organization, he changed this belief and asserted that an individual can be freed from bad karma by enduring various kinds of suffering.

In 1984 Asahara and his wife began holding yoga classes and in consequence soon gathered a following. In 1987 Asahara visited India and professed to have received 'final salvation' during a visit to the Himalayas. He began to set himself up as a messiah figure claiming that the Hindu god Shiva had personally commissioned him to establish the perfect society. On his return he continued to develop his organization, which he renamed Aum Shinrikyô (*aum* being a Hindu term signifying 'ultimate reality' and *shinrikyô* meaning 'the teaching of supreme truth'). In this year Asahara established headquarters at Fujinomiya in central Japan and also in Tokyo. Aum Shinrikyô's teaching was derived primarily from Hinduism and Buddhism. It also draws on Taoism and some passages of Christian apocalyptic writings.

In August 1989 Aum eventually succeeded in its bid to achieve legal recognition as a religious corporation. This gave it the opportunity to promote its activities and paved the way for Asahara and several other of the movement's leaders to offer themselves as Supreme Truth Party candidates for the House of Representatives. None of their twenty-five candidates was successful. The members of Aum felt this rejection keenly and in consequence came to the view that Armageddon was imminent. Asahara ordered his followers to build shelters and communes where they could escape from the outside world and its impending destruction. Possibly as early as 1990 he also gave instructions to Aum scientists to develop chemical weapons, including sarin gas, in order to protect the group.

In the summer of 1994 Aum developed its own form of government in direct opposition to Japanese rule with Shoko Asahara in the role of an imperial ruler. In the same year there was a serious gas leak at the Aum compound in the city of Matsumoto that caused considerable damage and resulted in the death of seven people. On 20 March 1995 ten prominent members of the group pierced bags containing sarin gas in five separate trains at Kasumigaseki station in the Tokyo subway. Twelve people died and 5,500 were injured. Asahara was arrested two months later at the movement's commune at the foot of Mount Fuji. In his subsequent trial in 1997 he pleaded not guilty, but in September 1999 the first of several death sentences for the Tokyo outrage was passed on other members. Asahara argued that it was legitimate to commit murder in certain circumstances because it is a way of preventing the person concerned from accumulating bad karma. He was sentenced to death by the Tokyo district court in 2004. A lengthy appeal is in progress.

In addition to the gas attacks there have been other deaths which the authorities connected with the movement. A Tokyo lawyer, Sakamato Tsutsumi, who had been investigating Aum, disappeared together with his wife and young child in November 1989 and their bodies were not recovered until 1995. Between 1988 and 1995 thirty-three followers were reported missing and presumed dead. In 1998 a Japanese court sentenced Kazuaki Okazaki to death by hanging for the murder of four people.

Core Beliefs

- Shiva, the Hindu god of creation and destruction, is held to be the chief deity.
- Yoga is practised as a means of overcoming bad karma.
- Meditation is followed as a means of achieving enlightenment in one lifetime.
- Armageddon (a major conflagration) will take place at the end of the world.
- The ultimate goal is to save all things living from transmigration.

Recent Developments

Asahara prophesied that, because of increasing and widespread evil, a nuclear war would erupt in 1999 which would culminate in the end of the world. He declared that only the salvation of 30,000 people would generate sufficient spiritual energy to avert this impending calamity.

In consequence of increasing government hostility, Aum changed its name to Aleph and finally distanced itself from Shoko Asahara, acknowledging that he may have been directly responsible for the gas attacks. Aleph, which is now led by Fumihiro Joyu, is working to compensate all the victims' families. They also required the entire following to reapply for membership, which included a declaration that they will obey the law. The Japanese government has not been convinced by these changes and Aum will remain under close surveillance until at least 2006, when the situation will be reviewed.

Aum claimed 10,000 members in 1995, but there are currently only an estimated 2,000 members in Japan of whom perhaps as many as 500 may be working in a full-time capacity. Many of the members were reported to have come from elite backgrounds. Following the terrorist attacks of September 2001 the US government froze the American assets of twenty-two groups, including Aum Shinrikyô.

Present Practice

The International Herald Tribune (25 March 1995) described Aum's training method as 'strenuous and exhausting, sometimes involving bizarre techniques'. One technique was a 'cleansing' procedure effected by drinking large amounts of water and then vomiting it up. To become a monk or a nun, all family ties must be renounced and the individual must donate all his or her assets to the group.

Within the movement's compound in 1995 daily life revolved around lengthy prayer sessions, some lasting for as long as four hours. During these times electronic headgear was sometimes used as it was thought to synchronize the participants' brain waves with those of Shoko Asahara. These 'brain hats', which can deliver a ten-volt shock, were also used in the 'Perfect Salvation' initiation ceremony. Life in Aum's communities was spartan with rough sleeping accommodation, periodic fasts and a minimal diet that frequently consisted of seaweed, burdock roots, radishes and carrots. The privileged were allowed to drink from the 'Miracle Pond', Asahara's bath water.

2.   The Bahá'í Faith

Origins

The Bahá'í Faith originated in Persia (now Iran) when Siyyid Ali-Muhammad (1819–50) who was the son of a cloth merchant began preaching that the Day of God was at hand. He became deeply interested in the Shia Islamic tradition of the Hidden Twelfth Imam who had escaped death at the hands of the Sunnis in 873 and disappeared from view. Shia Muslims differ from the Sunni majority on the matter of authority. They accept the Qur'an as their authority but accept only those traditions about the Prophet that have been recounted by his own household, including the twelve Imams. In contrast, Sunni Muslims also accept traditions concerning the Prophet which came from his disciples.

The Hidden Twelfth, who it is believed will rule the final age in secret, is a central end-time focus in Shiite Islam. In May 1844 after an extended period of prayer Siyyid proclaimed the 'Declaration of the Báb' asserting that he was the *Báb* (Arabic for 'gate') who had come to herald the arrival of The Hidden Imam (*Mahdi*), the one greater than himself who would fulfil the expectations of all the world's major religions and usher in a new era of universal peace and justice. Some scholars are of the view that Siyyid gradually became convinced that he himself was the Hidden Imam; yet others are of the view that he believed himself to have been the Hidden Imam from the very beginning. Regardless of these differing opinions, Bahá'ís view 1844 as the beginning of their religion. The Báb was an eloquent preacher and a gifted writer, soon attracting a large following who became known as Bábís. Siyyid instructed these new disciples and sent them out to proclaim the imminent coming of the Mahdi to establish the earthly kingdom of righteousness. The Shia authorities of Persia, who regarded his teachings as a threat to orthodoxy, were unimpressed and Siyyid endured harsh treatment, periods of imprisonment and finally execution by firing squad at the hands of Muslim clerics in 1850.

After enduring a lengthy gaol sentence and exile in Kurdistan, one of Siyyid's followers, the son of a government minister, Mírzá Husayn-Alí Nuri (1817–92), returned to take on the mantle of leadership of the Bábís in 1863, proclaiming himself the one the Báb had foretold, the *Bahá'u'lláh* (glory of God). Much of the rest of his life was an experience of suffering and hardship with periods of imprisonment and exile in various cities. He spent the last twenty years of his life near Acre, where in consequence the Bahá'í headquarters are located. During these years he preached and taught widely, declaring himself to be greater than the Báb and referring to himself as the Hidden Imam of the Shiites. He gained many thousands of followers and he lived his last years in considerable comfort supported by generous gifts of money. The Bahá'í scriptures clearly assert that Bahá'u'lláh is regarded as God.

After Bahá'u'lláh's death there were no further living prophets. He was succeeded by his son, 'Abdu'l-Bahá (1844–1921), and then his great-grandson, Shoghi Effendi Rabbání (1897–1957). Both made significant contributions to the faith, but were regarded simply as perfect human examples of his teachings.

The Báb wrote *Al-Bayan*. Bahá'u'lláh published a large number of letters and his books included a volume on spiritual guidance, *The Hidden Words* and *The Most Holy Book*, which contains laws for the new world order.

Core Beliefs

Although an offshoot of Islam, the Bahá'í Faith has a number of beliefs which set it apart from its parent organization, including a refusal to accept the supremacy of the Prophet Muhammad. The following are distinctive Bahá'í beliefs:

● There is only one God, who is the source of creation. God is known through a series of manifestations, the chief and most recent being that of Bahá'u'lláh.

● Bahá'ís do not accept a doctrine of sin but think only in terms of the misuse of good human qualities.

● God has sent and will continue to send prophets to the human race through whom the Holy Spirit has revealed the 'Word of God'. Great manifestations to the present era are:

1. Adam
2. Abraham
3. Moses (1456 BCE)
4. Krishna (1249 BCE)
5. Zoroaster (1200 BCE)
6. Buddha (757 BCE)
7. Jesus Christ (CE 34)
8. Muhammad (CE 613)
9. The Báb (CE 1844)
10. Bahá'u'lláh (CE 1863).

- All the great religions of the world share the same God and there is an essential unity between them.
- Every person has an immortal soul which at death is freed to progress through the spirit world.
- There will ultimately be a single world government based on Bahá'í's administrative framework.
- Heaven is regarded as a state of nearness to God, Hell as a state of remoteness from God.
- The individual's destiny is sealed as a result of his or her spiritual endeavours.
- The writings of the Báb and Bahá'u'lláh are regarded as scripture. Among the latter's most important works are *The Most Holy Book, The Hidden Words, The Book of Certitude, Gleanings from the Writings of Bahá'u'lláh*.

Recent Developments

When the Báb died, Bahá'u'lláh and his brother Mirza Yaha took on the leadership as a joint enterprise despite the fact that Mirza had been the Báb's choice as his successor. Two factions subsequently emerged with the majority following Bahá'u'lláh's announcement that he was the Mahdi and a small group (Azali Bábísm) following Mirza, believing themselves to be a movement within Shiite Islam. There are still small groups of Azali Bábis, mainly in Iran. The main Bahá'í group has not been altogether free of splinter groups and among them are *The New History Society* founded in New York in 1929 by Mirza Ahmad Sohrab and *The Bahá'í World Federation* founded in 1959 by Amin Effendi, Bahá'u'lláh's great-grandson.

In 1890 Dr George Kheiralla, a graduate of the American

College in Beirut, was converted to the Bahá'í Faith and subsequently travelled to the United States, eventually settling in Chicago. In a series of lectures he stimulated great interest in the Bahá'í Faith. Since then the religion has grown considerably. At the present time there are estimated to be 350,000 Bahá'ís in Iran, where they are regarded as heretics, and more than 5 million in 235 countries across the world.

Present Practice

Bahá'ís lay great stress on the ethical and social outworking of their Faith. Bahá'u'lláh laid down the following principles which he believed would help to unite the peoples of the world:

> 'Men must seek the truth in spite of custom, prejudice and tradition. Men and women must have equal opportunities, rights and privileges. The nations must choose an international language to be used along with the mother tongue. All children must receive a basic education. Men must make a systematic effort to wipe out all those prejudices, which divide people. Men must work to abolish extreme wealth and extreme poverty.'

The Bahá'í Faith therefore has a very strong humanitarian emphasis, rejecting all forms of racial prejudice and sexual discrimination. Members must abstain at all times from fault-finding and 'look always to the ten good qualities and not the one bad one'. This is based on Jesus' teaching in the Sermon on the Mount and on *The Hidden Words* of Bahá'u'lláh.

Bahá'ís stress the importance of healthy living. Alcohol and drugs are forbidden and vegetarianism is recommended in preference to the consumption of meat.

At the local level there are Spiritual Assemblies whose functions are defined in the writings of Bahá'u'lláh and Abdul-Bahá. Bahá'í has no priesthood and there are no liturgical services. Members are exhorted to pray in private each day and observe the nine holy days (which include the birth and martyrdom of the Báb and Bahá'u'lláh's declaration of his mission). They also fast from sunrise to sunset for a period of 19 days a year and work to abolish prejudice. They regard their work as a form of worship.

The movement is organized centrally and governed by The Universal House of Justice, which is staffed only by men.

Bahá'ís have a high view of science and scientific enquiry and do not accept that true religion and true science will be in conflict.

The ultimate goal for the Bahá'í is to find enlightenment, which is achieved by overcoming self and desire. By this means the light of divine presence will shine in each individual as it shone in Jesus Christ and in Moses and the Buddha. The Bahá'í Faith has wide appeal particularly to disenchanted adherents of the world's major religions.

3.   The Brahma Kumaris

Origins

The Brahma Kumaris ('the daughters, or girls, of Brahma') was founded by Dada Lekhraj (1876–1969), who was brought up within the traditions of Hinduism. The son of a village schoolmaster near Hyderabad, at that time in the British Indian province of Sind, he did not follow in his father's footsteps, but embarked on a career in the wheat trade and then the jewellery business, eventually amassing a considerable fortune as a diamond trader. Widely respected in his local community, he was well known for his charitable acts.

On reaching the age of sixty Lekhraj began to set aside more time for quiet and meditation. In 1936 over a period of several months he had a series of visions during which he had a revelation of God and of the process by which the world could be transformed. He believed that God, the Supreme Soul, had filled his very being. As a result he felt compelled to give up his business in order to follow his vision. Lekhraj began to teach that God lives in a world of light, which lies beyond the physical realm and is the home of all souls. He also believed the present age was a uniquely powerful era and that it was vital for individuals to seize the moment to work for the transformation of the world. In order to tap into this spiritual power, he urged his followers to move from body consciousness to soul consciousness. This did not require an austere life style or rejection of the physical world, but he did advocate the laying aside of material pursuits and the practice of celibacy. In 1937 he established the Brahma Kumaris World Spiritual Organization or Brahma Kumaris World Spiritual University (BKWSU) at Hyderabad. The following year the community of over 300 people moved to Karachi.

Dada Lekhraj remained the spiritual leader of the movement, leading and inspiring his students until his death at the age of ninety-three in 1969. His great wealth together with responsibility for the day-to-day leadership and organization of his followers he had handed over to a trust that he appointed in 1937 and which originally consisted of eight women. One of these 'founder girls' was Mateshwari Jagadamba Saraswati (1921–65), known as 'Om Radha' and 'Mamma' (mother), whose personal example and organizational talent contributed greatly to the growth of the movement.

After the partition of the subcontinent in 1947, Karachi was in West Pakistan (now Pakistan), and in the early 1950s the BKWSU headquarters moved to Mount Abu in Rajasthan, India, a quiet location in the Aravali Mountains. From here Dada Lekhraj, who became known as Brahma Baba (Revered God) and Pitashri Prajapita Brahma (Holy Father of Humanity), made a concerted effort to reach out to the whole of India.

Core Beliefs

Followers of the BKWSU, known as students, believe:
- that Lekhraj is a manifestation, some say an incarnation, of the Hindu god Shiva;

- that, although Lekhraj is dead, he still channels messages to them;
- in the return of Brahma Baba, at which point a destructive fire will end the present era and inaugurate a new Golden Age of spiritual power and ecological beauty;
- in the law of karma that asserts that our present actions influence our future life.

Recent Developments

After the early death of Mateshwari Saraswati in 1965, and the passing of Brahma Baba himself in 1969, the BKWSU was led into the twenty-first century by two other 'girls', now 'elder sisters', who had been among the founding eight: Dadi Prakashmani (b. 1922) in her role as Chief Administrative Head and Dadi Janki (b. 1916) as Additional Administrative Head. Dadi Prakashmani served on a number of international committees and for her outstanding contribution in the field of moral and spiritual education was awarded an honorary Doctor of Literature degree by Mohanlal Sukhadia University, Udaipur. She was also awarded the Peace Medal of the United Nations in 1981 in recognition of her endeavours to promote world peace. Dadi Janki was still inspiring meetings in England in 2005; for example, at Oxford town hall.

From the beginning in India in 1937 to 1971 the World Spiritual University activities were focused on serving the Asian continent and India and Pakistan in particular. In 1971 permanent centres were established in the UK and in Hong Kong. Present estimates indicate that the University has about 600,000 students in several thousand centres in over 80 countries, the majority of them in India. The University is now located in a new complex at Mount Abu called Madhuban ('forest of honey'), set among lakes and making use of solar and wind energy, from where the Brahma Kumaris centres worldwide are serviced. Mount Abu continues to be a centre of pilgrimage and attracts several hundred thousand people every year.

Present Practice

Devotees are encouraged not to harbour negative thoughts about Brahma Baba or the organization, as this reduces spiritual energy. New members are often given courses in 'positive thinking'. Members are also taught 'Living Values' of co-operation, humility, responsibility, freedom, love, happiness, peace, tolerance, honesty, respect and unity. By developing these qualities the individual will experience freedom from the influence of negative personality traits.

Brahma Kumaris emerged at the time of the partitioning of India and Pakistan and this contributed to its major stress on the importance of unity. While devotees wait for the arrival of the Golden Age, they are exhorted to strive for unity, recognizing that everyone, whatever their race, colour or creed, is a soul and needs to be treated as such. Members are encouraged to live humbly and yet confidently. They are to avoid material attachments and celibacy is a requirement.

Every Sunday afternoon Brahma Kumaris groups meet and take part in a meditation for peace and a message is given or the writings of Lekhraj are read.

4.   The Branch Davidians

Origins

The Branch Davidians emerged as a breakaway group from and retained many of the beliefs of the Seventh-day Adventists, whose dominant figure was Ellen White (1827–1915). They came into being during the years 1929–31 as the result of the teachings of Victor Houteff (1885–1955). Houteff, a Bulgarian emigrant, was an Adventist Sunday School teacher and lay preacher until his unorthodox views on the books of Daniel and Revelation caused the church to terminate his membership in 1929. Houteff moved to another part of Los Angeles and started his own separate organization that he called the Davidian Seventh-day Adventists. The group was popularly known as 'the Shepherd's Rod', the name being derived from a series of Bible studies by Houteff in 1930. The key teaching is that at the end time God will establish his literal kingdom in Israel, ruled by Jesus and his lieutenant, the antitypical David. Houteff's disciples soon began to see him as an inspired prophet and most went with him in 1934 when he purchased Old Mount Carmel Centre, a 300-acre settlement to the west of Waco, as a training centre for Bible study.

When Victor Houteff died, his widow Florence took the reins and declared that the end would take place in 1959. More than 1,000 Davidians from across the world gathered outside Waco at that time to await the final judgment day. They were expecting God to pick them up and take them to Israel. The prophecy failed to materialize and the majority of the members took off to form a variety of other groups. One was led by Benjamin Roden, who had just returned from a visit to Israel and announced himself as God's new prophet. In 1962 he succeeded in taking over New Mount Carmel, the former premises of The Davidian Seventh-day Adventists. Ben Roden introduced distinctive and significant teachings. God's people were to keep the biblical feast days (such as Passover, Pentecost, the Day of Atonement and Tabernacles) and were not to celebrate 'pagan' ones such as Christmas and Easter. Roden maintained that the scriptures that spoke of the 'Branch' referred to a distant future period and did not point to Jesus Christ. His contention was that the Branch was a modern day David who would come in the last days and deliver God's people. Roden died in 1978 and his wife Lois took on the leadership. One of her significant teachings was that the Holy Spirit is female. When she died in the later 1980s their son, George Roden, tried to establish himself as the Branch Davidian prophet but Vernon Howell ousted him.

David Koresh (1959–93) was born Vernon Wayne Howell in Houston, Texas, the illegitimate son of fifteen-year-old Bonnie Clark and Bobby Howell. His early life was difficult and his grandparents played a major role in the first years of his upbringing. In 1965 his mother married Ray Haldeman and took him back. His education was hindered by dyslexia, which prevented him completing his schooling. In later years Koresh described his most unhappy memory as the day he and a friend approached a group of fellow pupils who shouted out, 'Here come the retards.' His mother described him as 'a lonely fervently Christian child who would spend hours praying alone'.

Koresh later told his followers that he had been abused as a child. He had two assets, however: music and a passion for the Bible. Even at the age of twelve he had succeeded in memorizing many passages of scripture. For a while the young Howell worshipped with the Baptists, but at twenty he joined his mother's church, the Seventh-day Adventists. He had been with them for only two years when he was forced to leave on account of his bad influence on the church's young people. In 1981 he went to the Texas city of Waco, where he joined the Branch Davidians as a helper. Some time after his arrival he had an affair with Lois Roden, the Branch's leader and prophetess. He justified this relationship on the basis of the Old Testament book of Isaiah 8:3, 'And I went to the prophetess, and she conceived and bore a son.'

Lois Roden died in 1986 and her son George (1938–98) tried to take the reins and even renamed the compound 'Rodenville'. It was clear that he was emotionally unstable and members began to leave, fearful of what he might do. Eventually Roden lost out in a power struggle with Howell. In one episode Howell persuaded Roden to exhume the body of Anna Hughes, a former Davidian, to see which out of the two of them had sufficient divine power to raise it back to life. He then immediately succeeded in having Roden arrested for corpse abuse. George Roden was subsequently confined in a Texas mental hospital for the criminally insane after reputedly killing a man with an axe.

On becoming leader of the Davidians, Howell legally changed his name to David Koresh. (Koresh is a transliteration of the Hebrew word for Cyrus, the Persian king who paved the way for the Jews to return to Israel.) Once established at the helm of the movement, Koresh began a vigorous recruitment campaign and met with considerable success in England. Nearly half of those who later died in the Waco siege were from the UK. Koresh generated a considerable income by means of his business, which converted assault rifles into fully automatic machine-guns.

Core Beliefs

Branch Davidians

- share most of the orthodox Christian beliefs of the Seventh-day Adventists from whom they originated;
- believe they are God's chosen people chosen to survive Armageddon, the cataclysmic battle that will precede the end of the world;
- regard Ellen White, Victor Houteff, Ben Roden, Lois Roden and David Koresh as prophets and messengers from God;
- maintain that God is constantly revealing 'New Light' through these prophets (New Light drawn out from the scriptures so that the prophets demonstrate that it has been in the Bible all along);
- assert that true believers are those who believe and follow this 'Present Truth', with only these true believers being saved;
- believe that God has two revelations to humanity: one in Jesus Christ and the one at the end of time;
- believe David Koresh is the second messiah because he was able to explain the Seven Seals in the book of Revelation;
- believe that they will be greatly empowered in the last days by a special outpouring of the Holy Spirit that is the 'latter rain' spoken of by the Old Testament prophet Joel 2:23, the 'former rain' being the coming of the Holy Spirit at Pentecost.

Recent Developments

From 1990 David Koresh emerged as an increasingly dominant leader. He was strong and handsome. He played the guitar and always dressed like a faded rock star with jeans, cowboy boots and T-shirts. A Star of David earring dangled from one ear. He was a lucid speaker and could preach long sermons without the aid of notes; some of his Bible studies lasted for many hours. The strength of his personality was particularly apparent when his announcement in 1989, that he had the right to sleep with any woman so that he could spread his holy seed, was accepted. He justified this edict from Psalm 45:11–14 and from the Song of Songs 6:8, 'Sixty queens there may be and eighty concubines and virgins without number.' This, he claimed, entitled him to one hundred and forty wives, sixty 'proper wives' and 'eighty concubines'. In response, married male Branch Davidians who stayed gave up their wives to Koresh. Among his wives were a 67-year old widow and several teenagers. According to Jeannine Bunds, Koresh annulled the marriages of all couples that joined the group. He also demanded sexual tribute from women who joined and had sexual intercourse with girls as young as thirteen. Koresh sought to legitimate much of his behaviour by professing he had received prophecies. According to a former wife, Robin Bunds, Koresh was 'really nice' and humble; over the years, however, he lost a lot of those qualities and became in her words 'foul-mouthed' and pushy because of the power he had over his people. On one occasion he was reported to have spoken for an hour and a half on the evils of masturbation in a ranting sermon in which he used 'every gutter word' imaginable in front of a mixed group which included young children.

Once Koresh had let it be known that he was the Son of God,

he began increasingly to impress on his followers that they would face a final showdown with the authorities. He stockpiled vast quantities of food. He kitted them out in combat fatigues and trained them how to use a whole variety of weapons. Special agent Davey Aguilera, who took part in an eight-month surveillance discovered that Koresh had amassed a considerable arsenal of weapons which included machine-guns, a rocket launcher, an anti-tank machine gun, fifty 'pineapple' hand grenades and more than 1,800 rounds of ammunition. Koresh prepared his followers for battle by constantly making them watch Vietnam War films and by requiring them to take part in military-style drill and physical exercises. Among the films they were forced to watch was *Hamburger Hill* with graphic slow-motion pictures of US soldiers being shot to pulp by enemy machine-guns. Discipline was often harsh and visitors to the ranch and ex-followers say that some of the beatings lasted many minutes.

Tony Kakouri, a greengrocer's assistant from north London who spent six weeks at Mount Carmel in 1991, gave a harrowing account of life on the compound which echoed reports of escapees from other similar groups. Koresh used well-worn aggressive methods that included food and sleep deprivation, intimidation, isolation, violence, sexual abuse and long indoctrination sessions.

Koresh had succeeded in convincing his followers that he was the Son of God who alone was able to unlock the mystery of the Seven Seals described in the book of Revelation. He and his members were the only ones who would survive the imminent 'end times' and the moment would come when he would sit at the right hand of the Father. Events began to reach a head in February 1993 when the Bureau of Alcohol, Tobacco, and Firearms (ATF) forced their way into Mount Carmel in a search for illegal weaponry. Four ATF investigators were killed and others wounded including Koresh, who was hit in the wrist and in the waist. Six Davidians were believed to have died at the time, including Koresh's two-year-old daughter. From this point on Koresh increasingly feared that the authorities would come and arrest him and in consequence he formed his own group of guards known as 'the mighty men'. He maintained that, just as King David had established an elect bodyguard of 'mighty men', so it was necessary for him to do the same. By the beginning of 1993 they numbered twenty and they slept with their guns by their beds.

As a result of this debacle the FBI were called to the scene. What proved to be a fifty-one day siege began. The whole situation was poised for conflict with Koresh telling the FBI that he was waiting further instruction from God, preaching on the imminence of Armageddon and constantly referring to the compound as Ranch Apocalypse. To those who were with him at the end, his message was: 'Martyr yourselves. Go out, freak out, shoot and be shot, but kill many before you die.' He continued, 'If you can't kill for God, you can't die for God.' In a situation which uncannily paralleled Jesus Christ, also at the age of thirty-three, Koresh, the son of a carpenter, had had his side pieced by his enemies and was now waiting to die and rise again. The end finally came when the FBI fired CS gas into the compound that ignited an inferno that rapidly engulfed the entire complex killing David Koresh and almost all of his 108 disciples. The FBI took the view that the destruction was fault of the Davidians, but the nine members who escaped put the blame squarely on the FBI.

The Branch Davidians were reported as having twenty adherents at Waco in 2004 and claim to have fifty to a hundred followers worldwide.

Present Practice

At the present time there is still a small number of Davidians led by Clive Doyle (b. 1941), a Koresh follower who survived the Waco fire. Each Saturday he leads a cluster of disciples for Bible study. They believe that David Koresh will return and that a cataclysmic earthquake will befall the city. At the same time the shore of Lake Waco will drop, causing a devastating flood.

5.   The Christadelphians

Origins

The Christadelphians are a Bible-based lay movement whose members, roughly speaking, follow the teachings of their founder, Dr John Thomas (1805–71). Thomas, who was born at Hoxton Square, qualified with an MRCS from St Thomas' Hospital and practised medicine for two years at Hackney in the East End of London.

Early in 1832 his father, who at one point was minister at an Independent Congregational Church, was seized with the American emigration fever and John decided to go too, partly because of his intense dislike for what he termed 'the priest-ridden society of England'. After a traumatic Atlantic crossing the formerly agnostic Thomas attached himself to the Campbellites, an extreme Baptist group who followed the teachings of Alexander Campbell (1788–1868) and sought to recover the beliefs and practices of first-century Christianity. Thomas was baptized by one of their number by the light of the moon in the Miami Ship Canal, which led to the jibe that he had been 'moonstruck'. Thomas remained in association with the Campbellites until 1847, when he came to the view that 'we are saved by hope' (Romans 8:24) and that this hope is the coming of the Lord in power and great glory to set up a heavenly kingdom on earth, beginning at Jerusalem. This kingdom would not be 'beyond the skies', rather it 'would be in the Holy Land, when it shall be constituted a heavenly paradise'.

Having reached this new conviction, Thomas asked to be baptized again with the words: 'Upon confession of your faith in the things concerning the kingdom of God and the name of Jesus Christ, I baptize you in the name of the Father, Son and Holy Spirit.' Following this step of obedience Thomas published a lengthy confession, which included a section on this future hope.

Thomas found some initial support among the Campbellites in Baltimore and Buffalo, but his hearers in New York could not come to terms with the idea of the restoration of the Jews. In June 1848 Thomas returned to England and was well received in Nottingham and had further speaking engagements in Derby, Birmingham and Plymouth. He was particularly successful in Scotland. After a highly acclaimed campaign in Edinburgh he returned to London, where he wrote *Elpis Israel: An Exposition of the Kingdom of God*. This success in the British Isles is generally taken as marking the beginning of the movement. In 1862 he made a second journey to England and visited perhaps as many as fifteen major towns and cities. During this time he met Robert Roberts (1839–1898), whom he appointed to succeed him as overall leader. Roberts was an able speaker and writer who published a series of lectures under the title Christendom Astray. He travelled extensively both in the USA and in 1895 to Australia where he delivered 130 addresses and went on to New Zealand and Tasmania.

In 1872–73 Robert Roberts' own ecclesia in Birmingham drew up the *Birmingham Statement of Faith*, which was gradually adopted as their doctrinal basis by Christadelphian ecclesias all over the world. After Roberts' death there was a general tendency for Christadelphian ecclesias to go their separate ways. Christadelphians have never had any centralized council or organization. One important figure in recent times was John Carter (1889–1962), editor of *The Christadelphian* from 1937 to 1962. By his speaking and writing he was able to bring together many of the diversified groups and draw them into a more cohesive movement.

Core Beliefs

- God is a person but not a Trinity.
- Jesus is less than God: 'the simple appellation of "son" as applied to Christ, is sufficient to prove that his existence is derived and not eternal.'
- The Bible is uniquely inspired, 'a book of divine authorship', and is to be interpreted 'literally'.
- Sin is 'anything that opposes God and his commands'.
- Salvation is only possible through 'an exact knowledge of the will of God as contained in the scriptures, and faithfully carrying out the same'.
- Baptism is essential for salvation but can only be effective when the ideas of God and the future coming kingdom of God are understood.
- Salvation is essentially future when God's worldwide kingdom will be established on this earth with its administrative centre in Jerusalem. The Jews will be gathered in Palestine and the Kingdom of Israel will be restored. There will be a judgment, following which those who are 'true believers' will become immortal. Before all

this is established there will be a devastating conflict on the plains of Armageddon.

Recent Developments

There has been little change in doctrine and practice since the *Birmingham Statement of Faith* 1872–73. One or two of their more recent writers have speculated on the finer details of Armageddon, but generally speaking present-day Christadelphians avoid date setting and emphasize the need to live out Jesus' teaching faithfully so as to be found ready at his coming. There are approximately 300 ecclesias in the British Isles and membership is estimated to be of the order of 20,000. Circulation of *The Christadelphian* is more than 7,000 copies per issue with a slightly rising demand.

Present Practice

Christadelphianism is a lay movement. There are no clergy or ministers. Each local group is organized into a gathering known as an 'ecclesia' and is self-organized and self-governed. There is no central office and no attempt is made to compile statistics. Sunday morning worship is a breaking of bread and only members are allowed to attend. In the evenings there is a public meeting with a Bible lecture on some aspect of the kingdom. Each ecclesia has five presiding brethren, elected annually. They take it in turns to preside at the meetings.

Christadelphians maintain high standards of behaviour and, generally speaking, withdraw from places and activities that are considered to be 'of the world'. In more recent years, however, there has been a growing acceptance of entertainment and television. Certain occupations are closed to members because of the Christadelphian non-violent stance, including the police force, politics and the military. Marriage with a non-Christadelphian is not acceptable and leads to disfellowshipment.

6.   Christian Science

Origins

The origins of Christian Science are traceable to an American woman, Mary Baker Eddy (1821–1910), who bore this name following her marriage to Asa Gilbert Eddy on New Year's Day, 1877. Her parents, Mark and Abigail Baker, were devoted members of a Calvinistic Meeting House at White Rock Hill, New Hampshire. At the age of sixteen, Mary was admitted into membership of their Congregational Church at Sanbornton Bridge, New Hampshire. Mary's first marriage to George Glover, though happy, lasted only six months, George dying of yellow fever and leaving her to bear an infant son. The years which followed were a period of extended sickness and pain, compounded by the harsh and abusive treatment she received at the hands of her second husband, Daniel Patterson, whom she married in 1853. They were permanently separated in 1866 and in 1873 she obtained a divorce on grounds of his desertion.

During her second marriage Mary encountered Phineas P. Quimby (1802–66), whose remarkable healings were widely reported in the press. Quimby's system was based on creating wholesome moral attitudes in his patients. Under his treatment Mary made rapid progress and, despite having had severe 'spinal inflammation', in less than a week was able to climb the

182 steps to the dome of the City Hall. In February 1866 she fell on ice at a street corner in Lynn, Massachusetts, and appeared to have suffered some form of spinal dislocation. While lying flat on her back, she read the account of Jesus restoring the palsied man in Matthew 9. Quite suddenly she was filled with the sense that God was the only life and she was instantaneously healed.

Shortly after her healing Mary began to write out some simple principles that she had learned through her experience. As a way of supplementing her income she began in the summer of 1868 to offer classes in spiritual healing. In 1875, in order to better inform her students, Mary produced *Science and Health with Key to the scriptures*. Fundamental to Christian Science is the supposition that spirit is 'truth' and 'reality' whereas 'matter' is error and unreality. This did not mean material substances have no objective reality, as some critics of the movement mistakenly suppose. Rather, Mary's conviction was that because God is spirit, spirit is the ultimate and true reality. By contrast material existence is unreal. Furthermore, material substance and physical emotion can often mislead us and encompass what human beings perceive to be evil. As Mary saw it, the central aspect of personhood is not flesh, blood and bones but spirit. On this understanding physical pain and disease are not the ultimate reality or truth of the situation. If a person's mind and spirit can be positively influenced by allowing the divine spirit to embrace it, not only can the mind be changed to take on a positive wholesome outlook, the body can follow suit.

Mary has not been without her critics, some of whom have contended that *Science and Health* contained plagiarisms from Phineas Quimby and Francis Lieber (1800–72). Mary was undoubtedly influenced by Quimby, but the links with Lieber are harder to sustain. By 1877 Mary had come to the view that some sort of organization was necessary. In 1879 she established the First Church of Christ Scientist in Boston and two years later the Massachusetts Metaphysical College, which was closed in 1889. The following year the Boston church was renamed 'the Mother Church', so that it could manage the entire Christian Science Movement. Among other provisions it was laid down that 'the Bible and *Science and Health* were to be the sole pastors' of all churches of the Christian Science denomination, which has meant that no sermon is ever preached in Christian Science worship facilities.

Core Beliefs

Christian Scientists believe:

- that God is 'All-in-All', and they think of God in terms of 'Principle' rather than as a person; God is not a Trinity;
- that sin and evil have no objective reality: 'You conquer error by denying its reality';
- that sickness is an illusory condition of the mind and can be cured as the individual engages in silent prayer, adopting an optimistic outlook and focusing his or her thoughts on the Divine Mind;
- that the Bible is 'the inspired word' and 'our sufficient guide to eternal life' with *Science and Health with Key to the Scriptures* as an accompanying, major source of authority;
- that the human Jesus is distinct from Christ and merely revealed 'the spiritual Christ' to the world; that, because Jesus was endowed by the divine spirit without measure, he was able to be the mediator or 'Way-Shower' between God and men.

Recent Developments

Christian Science has tended to flourish in middle-class areas and among the more intellectual sections of the population. Its original values and practice have remained unchanged, in keeping with Mary Baker Eddy's earlier prescript. Many join on account of having received a healing through a practitioner. In Britain, where there were 158 places of worship in 2004, one-third of congregations were in the south-east of England. Estimates of world membership are between 350,000 and 450,000.

Present Practice

Mary Baker Eddy had a great dislike of ceremonial and things ecclesiastical and for this reason Christian Science has no clergy or full-time officials. Sunday worship is a quiet and meditative occasion with no dominant leader or president. The central focus is the reading of the lesson-sermon that consists of passages chosen from the Authorized Version of the Bible together with related sections from *Science and Health*. The lesson-sermon is given without any commentary or interpretation by two readers elected from the local membership. They cover 26 topics, each of which is covered twice a year. One of the readers leads the rest of the service, which includes hymns, silent prayer and the Lord's Prayer. There are no sacramental services and the Eucharist is regarded solely as a spiritual communion with the one God, the bread symbolizing truth and the cup the cross. Baptism is similarly regarded as purification from error and negative thoughts and motives. To become a Christian Scientist an individual has to subscribe to the 'Six Tenets of Christian Science' as laid down by Mrs Eddy and be sponsored by one, or in some cases, two members of the congregation. The use of alcohol and tobacco is a bar to membership. Healing is a very important aspect of Christian Science. To achieve status as a practitioner, a member must take a course with an 'authorized teacher of Christian Science'. There are currently more than 6,500 practitioners in 40 countries.

7. The Church of Jesus Christ of Latter-Day Saints (Mormons)

Origins

The Church of Jesus Christ of Latter-Day Saints, or Mormonism as the movement is often popularly called, was founded on 6 April 1830 by Joseph Smith Jr (1805–44), the third son of Joseph and Lucy Smith, at Fayette in New York State. Its present name was adopted in 1838. In 1823, following a series of visions, Smith was led to discover certain 'golden plates' on which were inscribed in 'Reformed Egyptian' the early history of the inhabitants of America and 'the fullness of the everlasting gospel'. Assisted by Oliver Cowdery, an itinerant school teacher, Smith translated the text and the *Book of Mormon* was published in 1830. In brief, it is the account of two great waves of emigration from the Holy Land to the American continent. The first of these left around the tower of Babel (c. 2250 BCE) sailing in eight barges. The civilization which they established provoked divine judgment and ended in destruction. The second wave and settlement, which began in 600 BCE, appeared to be more promising initially, with Jesus Christ visiting them in CE 34 and instituting the sacraments and giving a re-run of the Sermon on the Mount. History appeared to repeat itself, however, and strife and selfishness resulted in another total genocide. The last man to survive, Moroni, the son of Mormon, recorded these events on 'golden plates' and buried them in the hill of Cumorah in upper New York State. It was these that Smith located and began to translate in 1827. In 1835 he produced a second volume, entitled *Doctrine and Covenants*. This contained revelations regarding the Church's organization, priesthood and moral behaviour. It was accepted as Scripture.

Smith was a charismatic leader with a warm, outgoing disposition. His following, which expanded rapidly, moved with him first to Kirtland, Ohio, in 1835 and journeying on to settle at Nauvoo in Illinois. It was here that, as a result of their paramilitary activities, the Latter-Day Saints found themselves in conflict with the state authorities. On 12 July 1843 Smith announced the doctrine of polygamy, which resulted in considerable opposition in the columns of *The Nauvoo Expositor*. When on Smith's instructions his followers destroyed the press, he and his brother Hyrum were imprisoned in Carthage gaol where they were shot dead when an angry mob stormed the building.

Smith established the presidency of the church in 1843 and appointed himself first president. In 1844 he chose twelve apostles, including Brigham Young (1807–77). After Smith's death there was a brief struggle between Young and Sidney Rigdon for leadership, which resulted in Rigdon forming his own Church of Christ on 6 April 1845 and Young taking the Latter-Day Saints westward in the 'Great Trek' to Great Salt Lake Valley, Utah, where they settled in July 1847. It is estimated that 80,000 Mormons made the 1,300-mile journey.

A group led initially by Smith's first wife, Emma, felt that the leadership should have passed to Smith's son and separated from Young to form the Reorganized Church of Latter-Day Saints in 1860 with its headquarters and temple at Independence, Missouri.

Before Smith's death Mormon missionaries arrived in Britain at Liverpool in 1837 and by the following year there were 1,500 members and twenty congregations. British membership reached 30,000 in 1850.

On their arrival in Utah Young proved himself a masterly organizer. He set up a High Council of Twelve and a division into nine territorial wards. Salt Lake City was planned out with 135 blocks of ten acres. In 1890, when Wilford Woodruff was president, the Saints gave up the practice of plural wives that Smith had first officially announced in 1843. This enabled Utah to be granted statehood in 1896.

Core Beliefs

The core doctrines of the church are located in *The Articles of Faith* (thirteen in total) set out by Joseph Smith. Other doctrines were articulated by subsequent presidents. The following are noteworthy.

- 'We believe in God, the Eternal Father, and in His Son, Jesus Christ, and in the Holy Ghost.' (*Article 1*)
- 'Through the Atonement of Christ, all mankind may be saved by obedience to the laws and ordinances of the Gospel.' (*Article 3*)
- 'We believe the Bible to be the word of God as far as it is translated correctly; we also believe the *Book of Mormon* to be the word of God.' (*Article 8*)
- 'We believe in the literal gathering of Israel and in the

restoration of the Ten Tribes; that Zion (the New Jerusalem) will be built upon the American continent; that Christ will reign personally upon the earth; and that the earth will be renewed and receive its paradisal glory.' (*Article 10*)

● Jesus will return to establish a thousand-year reign of bliss, which will be followed by the final judgment when individuals 'will be assigned to the Kingdoms they earned by the way they have lived. The Celestial Kingdom is for the righteous only, the Terrestial Kingdom for those who did not hear the Gospel and the Telestial Kingdom for the wicked.' (*Doctrine and Covenants 76*)

● 'No man can ever enter the celestial kingdom without the consent of Joseph Smith.' (President Joseph Fielding Smith, *Doctrines of Salvation*, Volume 1, p.189)

● Marriage can be sealed for eternity in a special temple ceremony. (*Doctrine and Covenants* 132:15–18)

Recent Developments

The initial arrival of the Saints in Utah was coupled with a strong expectancy of Christ's imminent second coming, which was anticipated on American soil. Although with the passing of time this doctrine has been tempered, the LDS still has a strong millenarian expectancy which includes New Jerusalem being built on American soil.

In present-day Mormon organization there is at least one temple in each region where four main ordinances take place: baptism on behalf of those who have died without this sacrament, washings and anointings, endowments of priesthood and eternal marriage. Joseph Smith was himself a Freemason and for this reason these rituals bear a marked similarity to Masonic practice. LDS members in good standing are able to go to the temple where they can be washed and anointed and this enables them to achieve exalted status in the celestial (or third) heaven.

Since the nineteenth-century beginnings the Latter-Day Saints have expanded their numbers rapidly. Today their churches can be found on every continent and their global membership is growing at approximately 5 per cent a year. Worldwide membership is 10.2 million, with the majority in the USA and Canada. In Britain there are 185,000 members and 430 places of worship.

Present Practice

The Church of Latter-Day Saints has a developed structure. The head of the church is the president and chief prophet, who is always the longest serving and therefore the most senior of the apostles. The president holds office for life and is expected to receive fresh revelations from God. For administrative purposes the world is divided into twenty areas, with each area then split into smaller regions which in turn are subdivided into stakes. Within each stake there are individual congregations known as 'branches' or 'wards'. The 'Stake Presidency' consists of three men who are 'called to office' rather than chosen.

Sunday worship consists of Bible study and instruction and a sacramental meeting with bread and water rather than wine. There are two levels of priesthood. The Aaronic priesthood is open to boys over twelve years of age and enables them to bless and pass on the sacrament. The Melchizedek priesthood is for men over nineteen years of age and is more concerned with spiritual matters, such as visiting the sick and administering the laying on of hands.

Latter-Day Saints place strong emphasis on welfare and large sums are raised through Fast Offerings, through which members pay the cost of two meals a month into a fund for the poor. There is also a pronounced campaign of evangelism, and a high percentage of young Mormons undertake a two-year missionary journey at their own expense. LDS give high priority to the family and every Monday evening is a family night, with all members expected to spend the evening in family and fund activities. In accordance with their *Doctrine and Covenants* (89: 5, 7–9), all Latter-Day Saints abstain from tobacco, alcohol, tea, coffee and hot drinks.

(Recent revelations to the president of the off-shoot Reorganized Church of Latter-Day Saints resulted in the ordination of women in 1985; and in 2001 the organization, which has come closer to mainstream Christian doctrine, was renamed the Community of Christ.)

8.   The Church of Scientology

Origins

Scientology is a system devised by Lafayette Ron Hubbard (1911–86). In his words it means 'knowing in the fullest sense' and, to help people achieve this, it 'provides a route that can show you where you are'. 'The end result of Scientology studies and drills,' Hubbard wrote, 'is a renewed awareness of self as a spiritual and immortal being.' This scheme Hubbard set out in his book, *Dianetics: The Modern Science of Mental Health*, published in 1950 and quickly selling over a million copies. Hubbard was born in the Nebraska town of Tilden, but spent much of his childhood in Montana. He attended George Washington University for two years, but did not complete his civil engineering degree. Although he was unsuccessful in physics, Hubbard developed a very successful career as a science fiction writer in the 1930s and 40s. But it was the publication of *Dianetics* which brought him world renown. This volume became the sacred text for the religion which he inaugurated in Los Angeles in 1954.

Hubbard, who claimed to have visited heaven on two occasions, established the movement's headquarters at Saint Hill Manor in East Grinstead, Sussex, England, though it later moved to California. From 1965 he spent part of each year in the UK and the rest in a 300-foot ship named *Apollo* together with the Sea Org, a group of his top-class recruits. He spent a total of about ten years at sea, mostly in the Mediterranean or off the eastern Atlantic coast of America. During that time the Sea Org, many of whom were young, served him with devotion, cooking his meals and washing his clothes. In the later 1970s he disappeared from view and spent part of his time on a replica of a life-size clipper which he had constructed at Gillman Hot Springs on the edge of the Mojave Desert. So secluded was his existence that one of his sons, Ronald De Wolf, who had changed his name after disowning his father, petitioned a California court to be designated a trustee of his father's estate.

Scientology contends that the human mind is divided into two, with an analytical function and a reactive function. The analytical part of the mind perceives, remembers and conducts the reasoning processes and resolves problems. The reactive mind is more passive and subconsciously receives and stores harmful experiences called 'engrams'. Although people are not aware of it, engrams damage their mental health, which in turn may affect their physical and emotional well-being. When a person is fully conscious, the analytical mind is in command of the situation; but when an individual is only partially conscious perhaps as a result of grief, pain, shock or illness, the reactive mind cuts in. Every harmful memory and mental picture (or engram) is stored away, resulting in emotional damage. The aim of the Scientology's 'drills and studies' is to remove all the engrams from the client. A person who has been completely cleared of them is designated 'a Clear'.

In order to identify engrams, Scientology practitioners, referred to as Auditors, engage 'pre-clears' in a series of counselling sessions. During these meetings the auditors use a battery-operated 'E-meter' (electropsychometer). In essence this device consists of two small cylinders which the counselee holds in either hand. The thinking is that when the auditor touches on an emotionally sensitive area of the client's life, his or her body temperature and pulse-rate will change and cause the meter needle to move up the scale. This is taken to indicate the presence of an engram, which can be eliminated by further counselling or drills. Essentially it is by confronting the problem/engram that the person's 'memory bin' is cleared.

Individuals often make their first acquaintance with the Church of Scientology when they are met on the streets or read an ad in a magazine or leaflet offering *The Oxford Personality Test* free of charge. The results are often shown to the individuals concerned on a printout in the form of a graph. They are then urged to take the counselling course which will enable them to be freed from the engrams which lie dormant within them. In Hubbard's words, 'The *clear* is the goal in Dianetic therapy, a goal which some patience and a little study and work can bring about.' These courses are quite costly. In the USA the fees to become a Clear can be upwards of $4,000. Beyond 'clear' there is a whole series of higher levels which can be undertaken, such as 'The Clear Certainty Rundown'. These are more expensive and culminate in 'The Bridge to Total Freedom'.

Core Beliefs

- Belief in a supreme being. Hubbard's Eighth Dynamic is 'the urge towards existence as infinity. This is also identified as the Supreme Being.'
- A person's true self is not their body or mind but their spiritual self or thetan (pronounced 'thaytan').

● The problem for all human beings is that the thetan becomes encrusted with painful engrams. Some of the most negative engrams, according to Hubbard, come as prenatal experiences which he termed 'contra-survival engrams'. He gave the example of a father hitting a mother in early pregnancy, which later causes the child pain and may result in his or her dramatizing or acting out that pain or the hurt done to the mother. Hubbard also taught that engrams could be inherited from previous lives.

● Salvation is achieved when the thetan is totally cleared of engrams.

● The harmful effect of the engrams can be removed from any person 'unless he has been so unfortunate as to have had a large portion of his brain removed'. This is accomplished by auditing, which is effected by means of counselling and the use of an E-meter.

● Once the state of 'Clear' has been realized, individuals can go on to explore other worlds and ultimately reach their full potential as gods.

Recent Developments

Somewhat like the multimillionaire recluse Howard Hughes, Hubbard disappeared almost entirely from view in 1980 and only a small group of his most trusted aids, not including his wife, had any contact with him. During that time Hubbard devoted his energies to writing a best-selling science fiction epic, *Battlefield Earth*, and a ten-volume series entitled *Mission Earth*. This was a bleak period for the Church of Scientology, with bad publicity surrounding the Guardian's Office (GO). David Miscavidge eventually closed down GO and a new administrative structure was established.

In 1993 the church achieved a major breakthrough when it was granted tax-exemption status as a religion by the US Internal Revenue. In Britain the Home Office recognized it as a religion in 1996. Some people regard it simply as a system of behaviour or psychotherapy rather than a religion.

By 1968 the movement had thirty-eight churches in the USA and a further 41 in other countries; there were 172 'missions' and an estimated 5.5 million adherents. When Hubbard died in 1986 his movement was estimated to have 3 million members. The church states that there are currently more than 3,200 churches, missions and groups in 156 countries. What this represents in terms of active participant members is hard to estimate. In 1994 membership was given as 100,000 for the UK, but this probably included large numbers of individuals who attended some form of counselling or therapy at a Scientology centre. The 1996 Australian census reported an estimated membership of 4,000 with 500 in full-time service. Worldwide the number of full-time Scientologists may be 9,000 to 10,000. Outside the USA, Scientology appears most active in Germany. Today the Sea Org is the top level of the church's organization. They hold the senior appointments in the ecclesiastical hierarchy and the major positions in PR and technical areas. Following Hubbard's death in 1986 the leadership passed to David Miscavidge.

Present Practice

Each local Scientology church has a chaplain who conducts Sunday services that are open to anyone of any denomination.

During these times of worship there are no references to God and no prayers. There are rites for the equivalent of baptism as well as marriage and funeral services which are led by the church's clergy. There are also special celebration days which approximate to the Catholic church's saints days. Ron Hubbard's Birthday is 13 March and 12 August is Sea Org Day, commemorating the establishment of the Sea Org. Scientology churches are open each day of the week for counselling, advanced courses and social activities.

The majority of active Scientologists are from middle-class backgrounds and many are in managerial and professional positions. Scientology has counted a number of high profile personalities among its adherents. They include John Travolta, Tom Cruise and Priscilla Presley. Their presence and commitment has undoubtedly helped to increase interest in the organization's programmes.

Scientology has been active in a number of education and social programmes, most notably drug education through its Narconon centres.

9. The Church Universal and Triumphant (Summit Lighthouse)

Origins

The Church Universal and Triumphant was originally founded as the Summit Lighthouse by Mark L. Prophet (1918–73) in Washington, DC, in 1958. The church's basic teachings were developed from the 'I AM' movement that began in the teachings of Guy Ballard (1878–1939) and his wife Edna (1886–1971) in the early 1930s and were set out in Guy's book *Unveiled Mysteries* (1934).

'I AM', which is borrowed from the book of Exodus 3:14, has its roots in early gnostic thinking, Eastern mysticism, theosophy and Christianity. Its basic contention is that certain enlightened spiritual beings who once lived on earth have ascended to their divine source. They can now connect with people on earth and guide and bring them into conscious touch with God. Chief among these 'Ascended Masters' were Jesus and a seventeenth-century occultist, the Comte de Saint Germain, with whom Ballard claimed to have had direct encounter in 1930 on Mount Shasto in California. Ballard recounted this meeting in a book entitled *Unveiled Mysteries* that he published in 1934. Saint Germain informed Ballard that he had gone through a series of reincarnations, one of which was George Washington, and had finally achieved the position of Ascended Master. When Ballard died, his wife took on the leadership and announced that her husband was now an Ascended Master.

Mark Prophet, who was a theosophist, was for some years involved in an 'I AM' offshoot, The Bridge to Freedom Church, before founding his own Summit Lighthouse. The aim of his new organization was to publish the revelations he claimed to have received from an Ascended Master, El Morya, who had first contacted him when he was seventeen. In 1963 Mark Prophet married Elizabeth Clare Wulf (b. 1939), who came from a Lutheran background, was a kindred spirit, had participated in some of his early conferences and shared his vision. Mark saw himself as the mouthpiece for the Ascended Masters, collectively referred to as the Great White Brotherhood because of the white light surrounding their forms. On 5 July 1964 it was announced that his wife had received the mantle of messenger of the Great White Brotherhood and would be sharing his work of channelling messages of guidance and help to humanity.

In 1966 they moved to Colorado Springs, the first of several relocations. In 1972 the Prophets co-authored the organization's major text, *Climb the Highest Mountain*. In 1973, following Mark's death, Elizabeth Prophet assumed the leadership, changed the organization's name to The Church Universal and Triumphant (CUT) and on the basis of received dictations declared herself to be the sole representative of the Great White Brotherhood. Not long afterwards she married Randall King and relocated the headquarters to a former Roman Catholic monastery.

In 1975 the church published an important document, *The Chela and the Path*, which it claimed was directly from El Morya.

It asserted that Mark and Elizabeth Prophet were part of a long line of messengers extending back through the Ballards and the Comte de Saint Germain to Mary Baker Eddy (*see* Christian Science) and Helena Blavatsky (*see* The Theosophical Movement). These and other individuals have overcome all negative karma and so have ascended back to be reunited with the divine spirit.

CUT has a typically Gnostic view of humanity. The physical body is a lower, changing being but contained within it there is a divine spark which is part of a higher, unchanging being. By seeking messages, light and help from the Ascended Masters the power of the higher self is gradually able to transform the individual's physical nature. This continuous transformation takes place during a series of reincarnations. Ultimately, individuals will realize the potential of the Christ within them and ascend to God as Christ did. One of the church's major articles of belief is: 'We proclaim the Church Universal and Triumphant, founded by Almighty God on the rock of Christ Consciousness.' This is no quick process; the path to the summit of the lighthouse is steep.

In addition to receiving messages from spiritual beings who have purified themselves, the CUT also practises a form of prayer known as 'decreeing'. This amounts to the individual making positive statements as though they were already facts.

Core Beliefs

● God is an all-pervading spirit and does not exist apart from the universe. This is essentially Hindu pantheism.
● God is the source of all that is.

- God possesses male and female characteristics and is referred to as 'Father-Mother'.

- Jesus Christ is understood as two separate concepts. Jesus was a historic person who lived and taught in Judea. Christ is the principle of divine consciousness that Jesus was able to achieve. CUT does not accept that Jesus was both fully human and fully divine; rather, Jesus is one of the Ascended Masters and can be worshipped as such. Jesus did not die as sacrifice for sin but to overcome bad karma.

- The Holy Spirit is seen as an impersonal energy or force whose function is to fill all things with the knowledge of God.

- Men and women consist of a lower, physical self and a higher, spiritual self. By overcoming bad karma a person's higher nature may transform the lower nature so that ultimately he or she may achieve divine status.

- The church is the 'I AM' race which consists of all those who are following the teachings of the Ascended Masters.

- Members of CUT believe that Armageddon is imminent (and at one time constructed bomb shelters on their Montana estate headquarters to enable them to survive the coming conflagration).

- The Ascended Masters are enlightened spiritual beings who once lived on earth but now have ascended to their divine source. Together they are the Great White Brotherhood. Many Ascended Masters have chosen to connect with souls on earth to guide and help them to reunite with the divine consciousness.

- Angels are spiritual beings who interact with people on earth. They exist in myriads and serve the human race 'in just about every capacity imaginable, from helping us to tend to the care and health of our body, to finding parking spaces, passing tests, mending relationships, cleaning up oil spills and stopping wars'. Angels are believed to affect people and the creation with intensely positive feelings and vibrations.

● Prophecy is messages received from the Ascended Masters. These are often warnings to which individuals can respond and they thus bring about a change in the course of events.

● Mark and Elizabeth Prophet are not Ascended Masters but are regarded as messengers of God.

Recent Developments

After several relocations within California, the church established its current headquarters on a 32,000-acre ranch in Montana, north of Yellowstone Park, in 1986. It became a major focus of attention when Elizabeth Prophet declared that the Soviet Union would launch a major missile attack on the USA on 23 April 1990 and members from across the world paid up to $12,000 dollars a head for a place in one of the bomb shelters built by the church's staff. She subsequently revised this prediction, stating that the date in question simply marked the beginning of a dozen years of negative karma against the organization. The Montana state authorities have banned the church from using the shelters again.

CUT received adverse publicity for storing 650,000 gallons of fuel at its ranch in 1990 and for purchasing and allegedly stockpiling weapons. The latter issue came to a head when Elizabeth Prophet's fourth husband, who was then the church's vice-president, was sent to prison for using the name of a deceased Aids patient to purchase military equipment. This led to Mrs Prophet's divorcing him, despite her having previously announced that the marriage had been divinely inspired.

The church's membership has fallen significantly from its estimated peak of 10,000.

Present Practice

The members of CUT are predominantly conservative-minded members of the middle-class aged between thirty and sixty. A significant number have advanced degrees and regard education as a high priority. Those who are full communicant members commit themselves to abstaining from alcohol, tobacco and other drugs. The church regards diet as an important issue and recommends limited eating of red meat. Elizabeth Prophet was reported by Cathleen Mann, a former member, to have exercised strict controls, which included approving dating, marriage and the frequency of sexual relationships. No red, black or orange clothing was to be worn; no sugar, soft drinks, chocolate or coffee were allowed and carrots were declared to be 'the food of the masses'. A board of directors runs the church and it is expected that they will continue to do so when Mrs Prophet is no longer able to play a role.

10.   Eckankar

Origins

Eckankar (which means 'worker with God') is a system with roots in Hinduism, Christianity, Sikhism and Spiritism. It was first devised by Paul Twitchell (1908–71), who claimed to be in direct descent from the ancient, many would say mythological, civilization of Atlantis.

Twitchell was born in Kentucky and together with his elder sister, Kay-Dee, learned the principles of soul travel from Sudar Singh, whom they met in Paris, possibly in 1940. They travelled to India and studied at his ashram for a year. Twitchell studied at Western State Teachers' College at Western Kentucky University and he later joined the US Navy. Before founding Eckankar in 1965 he also earned a living as editor and later correspondent for *Our Navy* magazine. His religious experiences included membership of The Self-Revelation Church of Absolute Monism, from which he was expelled in 1955 allegedly for unacceptable behaviour. This was followed in the same year by his initiation into Ruhani Satsang, a splinter group arising out of the Radhasoami Tradition (in the larger Sant Mat tradition) started by Kirpal Singh (1894–1974), who taught a form of meditation focused on the energy that is within an individual. This experience was to be crucial, since the basics of Eckankar's teaching are very similar to sound current yoga (*see also* Elan Vital). Twitchell's second wife, Gail, was also initiated into Ruhani Satsang in 1963. In 1958 Twitchell joined the Church of Scientology and for a while was even on the staff.

'Eck' is believed to be an emission from the high God, a current on which the soul can travel through the universe and explore other planes of spiritual existence. Adherents aim to get their soul to reach Sugmad, the ocean of love and mercy, the divine source. There is a Living Master who guides the Eckist devotee or 'chela' to other planets by means of astral projection. It was Twitchell's view that many of the world's great religious leaders taught astral projection. In his writing he contended that Jesus and other Bible characters were among those who made use of soul travel. In his book *Eckankar: The Key to Secret Worlds* (1969) he wrote: 'According to the Gospels, Jesus said, "Come and follow me." ' But few knew he was saying that he wanted them to go with Him into the worlds beyond. They were not prepared to make the journey.'

Twitchell asserted that he had been initiated by a group of spiritual masters, who had assigned him the role of 971st Living Eck Master.

Core Beliefs

● God is in all things.
● Kal Niranjan, king of the Lower Worlds, is a lesser-evil deity identified with Jehovah, who inhabits the lower physical realm. He is the source of negative energy in the universe.
● Jesus, as the son of Kal, is identified with evil power in the world.

- The entire world is a prison in which the human race is trapped.
- The soul is eternal and lives independently of the material body.
- Individuals are held in bondage in the present world by religions and philosophies.
- By means of astral projection the soul is able to exert its independence from the body.
- There is a series of eleven planes between the physical plane and the highest plane that is Sugmad.
- The kingdom of heaven is the upper six of the eleven cosmic layers in the universe.
- It is not possible to enter the kingdom of heaven except through the teachings of Eckankar.

Recent Developments

After Twitchell's early death in 1971 the leadership passed to Darwin Gross (b. 1928), a musician born in Denho, North Dakota. Gross married Twitchell's widow, Gail (although they divorced in 1978). Gross transferred the administrative offices to California and Eckankar continued to grow despite accusations that its teachings were substantially those of Ruhani Satsang and other Sant Mat groups. Gross's authority was not widely accepted and in 1981 he handed the mantle of leadership on to Harold Klemp (b. 1942), who became the 973rd Living Eck Master. Klemp moved the headquarters to Minneapolis, Minnesota, where he oversaw the building of the Temple of Eck, which opened in 1990. Approximately 5,000 members attend Eckankar's annual October worldwide conference in Minnesota. Eckankar currently claims a membership of 50,000.

Present Practice

Eckankar is a living and evolving religion that always regards the teachings of previous Eck Masters as being of less significance and importance than the present one's. The central aspect of Eck belief is that souls can ascend through a series of eleven planes to the kingdom of heaven, where God is. Twitchell taught that the first five planes are physical and the remaining six are spiritual. The ultimate goal is to reach the upper plane of the heavenly or spiritual realm, known as Sugmad. Each time the devotee ascends to a higher level there is a special initiation ceremony. Once the devotees reach Sugmad, they can look forward to becoming one of God's co-workers and assisting in the running of the universe. In essence salvation is therefore the realization of the presence of God.

Each of the eleven planes is believed is to be recognizable by its particular sound. In order to travel up through these realms the chela must seek out a spiritual guide, known as an Eck Master. The major techniques employed to facilitate soul travel or out-of-body experiences are imaginative projection, meditation, projection through the dream state, trance and willing one's consciousness to be in another location. Eck devotees also frequently chant special mantras.

11.   Elan Vital

Origins

In the West in the 1960s, when there was a growing disenchantment with Western values, large numbers of young people in particular began to be attracted to the teachings of Eastern gurus. One of these was Sri Hans Maharaj (1900–66), who founded Divine Light Mission in India in 1960. His teaching was based on the Hindu concept of enlightenment through knowledge. When Sri Hans Maharaj died, his eight-year-old son, Prem Pal Singh Rawat (b. 1958), caused astonishment by announcing that he was to be the new guru, Maharaji. According to some reports, in 1971, when he was still only thirteen, he received a revelation that he was to be the saviour of the world. In that same year he announced himself as 'Perfect Master' and, while his mother and elder brother, Bal Bhagwan Ji (b. 1951) effectively controlled Divine Light Mission in India, he commenced a world tour with the aim of establishing a movement in the USA and Britain. In England he attended the Glastonbury Rock Festival and briefly took the stage to offer his services.

The following year marked the beginning of a highly successful period in which Maharaji succeeded in making 2,000 converts at Montrose, Colorado. He was hailed as the 'Lord of the Universe' and 'The Perfect Master' and thought by some to be the successor of Jesus and the Buddha. In the following year a 'Millennium 73' event was held at the Houston Astrodome to launch a spiritual millennium of a thousand years of peace. There some 20,000 people worshipped Maharaji as he sat high above them on a suspended throne. Overall, 'Millennium 73' did not recruit well and incurred a financial loss of $600,000. However, the American Divine Light Mission (later to become Elan Vital) continued to grow and Maharaji's international headquarters were set up in Denver, Colorado.

In 1974, when he was only sixteen, Maharaji married his secretary, Marolyn Johnson, a former airline stewardess, and renamed her Durga Je after an Indian goddess. This caused a further decline in his relationship with his mother, Mati Ji, who had already expressed her anxieties regarding his opulent lifestyle. When she arrived in Malibu, California, to see him, she was allegedly prevented from entering his estate by his new bride. In a public outburst of anger she denounced him and appointed his brother Bal Bhagwan Ji leader of the movement, which she renamed the Spiritual Life Society.

As a result Maharaji severed his links with India and many of his Indian assistant teachers were dismissed and returned home. He also stressed that the basis of his teaching was universal rather than Indian. From this time onwards Maharaji's following declined. Many began to be puzzled that the new messiah had taken up residence in the USA. Others, who noted the young guru's taste for extravagant food, large houses and expensive cars, especially Rolls Royces, felt they had been misled. By the mid-1970s Maharaji was conscious that many were leaving his movement and began to revert to some of the older Indian customs. In 1977 and 1978 elaborate costumes and dance were introduced into many of his public programmes.

Core Beliefs

A number of Divine Light's basic teachings derive from Hinduism. However, Maharaji's teachings follow the wisdom tradition, which requires no authentication through scripture and permits renewal under the guidance of a living master. Some parallels can be found among such figures as the founder of Sikhism, Guru Nanak (1469–1539), Kabir (a fifteenth-century Indian sant) and Jalal al-Din Rumi (1207–73), a Persian Sufi poet and founder of a Dervish order. Currently Maharaji's teachings include:

● Maharaji is a divine incarnation.
● Human beings are inherently good.
● True knowledge which enables devotees to discover the divine self that is within every human being is received directly from Maharaji.
● The process of receiving true knowledge is enhanced by a form of yoga known as *Siddha*.

Maharaji's five commandments are:
1. Refrain from postponing till tomorrow what can be done to day.
2. Always meditate on the holy name.
3. Never doubt.
4. Never avoid attending satsang (here: a gathering for teaching).
5. Always have faith in God.

Recent Developments

By the mid-1970s Maharaji's following had fallen from an estimated figure of 50,000 to about 7,000. In addition, there were still followers of his father's original Divine Light, now run by Bal Bhagwan Ji. In 1979 Maharaji's headquarters were moved from California to Miami, Florida, but reverted to Malibu after only a short period.

The 1980s were a turning point for Maharaji's organization. In 1983 he ordered the closure of all the ashrams. At the same time the organization was renamed Elan Vital (French for 'vital spirit') with the plain objective of making available the teachings of Maharaji. Its ethos became increasingly Westernized, with Maharaji opting for Western-style suits in place of traditional Indian dress. A British arm of EV was established in 1991 and registered as an educational charity the following year. The current number of Maharaji's followers (known as Premies, meaning 'lovers of God') is hard to estimate. Maharaji's web page reported an average monthly attendance of 472,230 in 1998; in that same year 'Knowledge' was given to 20,387 people. In 2000 a worldwide estimate of 335,000 was put forward. Elan Vital itself keeps no membership figures, but stated to the author in 2005 that 'in 2004 alone 1.4 million people came to hear Maharaji speak in different countries around the world' and 'more than 500,000 to this day have learned the techniques [called Knowledge]'.

Present Practice

Maharaji now lives in the USA with his wife and four children. He alone spreads the true knowledge, which he does by distributing videos, audio tapes and various kinds of literature. He spends the bulk of his time writing articles setting out Elan Vital's teaching and travelling the world to give lectures and seminars. His main theme is the way in which individuals can know peace and contentment in the present. This knowledge is achieved by means of sound current yoga and meditation using Divine Light, Divine Music, Divine Nectar and Divine Word. Divine Light meditation is a technique in which the eyes are closed, so that the focus is on the inside; Divine Music is achieved by placing the underside of the thumbs lightly over the ears but not over the cartilage piece and this produces the Music; Nectar is focusing on breathing; and Divine Word is a technique in which the tongue is made to vibrate on the palate. When an individual is ready to receive this knowledge, he or she is initiated in a lengthy ceremony which takes place in a darkened room. Many practitioners report a remarkably increased awareness of the realities around them. EV members use the major Hindu scriptures as the main source of their devotional reading. In general terms the present emphasis of Elan Vital is much less focused on Maharaji and much more on his teaching and quest to find peace within.

12. The Exclusive Brethren

Origins

The roots of Exclusive Brethrenism are traceable to John Nelson Darby (1800–82), the youngest son of John Darby of Leap Castle, Kings County, Ireland. His uncle was a personal friend of Admiral Lord Nelson. Darby studied law at Trinity College, Dublin, and was called to the bar in 1822. On being 'converted' he took orders in the Anglican Church of Ireland, becoming Curate of Calany, a remote parish in County Wicklow. During a period of convalescence in 1827 Darby came into contact with a group of discontented upper-class evangelicals who were experimenting with informal breaking of bread (communion) services in Dublin. Among their number were Edward Cronin (1802–82), Anthony Norris Groves (1795–1853), a dentist, and John Gifford Bellett (1795–1864), a lawyer. The group expanded into what became the first Brethren assembly.

Darby did not return to his parish, finally leaving the established church and becoming instead the dominant figure of this select circle. He was an inveterate traveller and early on visited both Cambridge and Oxford, where he met George Vicesimus Wigram (1805–79), a distinguished academic, whose brother Joseph became Bishop of Rochester. Meetings were established in many places, including London and Bristol. It was, however, at Plymouth, Devon in 1847 that the split occurred which resulted in the formation of the Exclusives. The newly formed Plymouth assembly was led by Benjamin Newton (1807–99), a fellow of Exeter College, Oxford, and a former Church of England layman. It came to light that Newton had been covertly teaching what the Brethren later termed 'the tainted Christ', in which he maintained that Jesus had, like the rest of the human race, been born under the curse of God and remained so until the time of his baptism in the River Jordan. Some of those who sat under Newton's teaching soon acknowledged its error, as indeed did Newton himself. Darby, however, maintained that those who had listened to Newton were 'tainted' and insisted on separation from all who had fellowship with Newton.

When some of their number went to the Bethesda Assembly in Bristol and were allowed to break bread, Darby called on the leaders to exclude them, maintaining there was evidence that some of them had accepted Newton's teaching. They declined and instead issued *The Letter of the Ten* in June 1848, which committed Bethesda to the original Brethren position of keeping the communion table 'open' to all who share the historic, biblical, Christian faith. In response Darby issued his celebrated *Bethesda Circular* the same year, in which he maintained that to associate with evil 'is opening the door to the infection of the abominable evil'. This, in the words of Canon Gordon McPhail, led on to 'the fundamental idea of Brethrenism as it exists today, that of "the ruin of the Church"'.

From 1849 the Exclusives emerged as a separate group from the Open Brethren (who as a consequence of this chapter in their history were sometimes referred to as Plymouth Brethren) and the Exclusives expanded into Europe, the USA and Canada, as

Darby travelled and preached and George Wigram edited their journal under the title of *The Present Testimony*. Darby divided biblical history into seven periods which included the pre-millennial second coming of Christ. His scheme was taken up by a number of American evangelists and popularized at prophetic Bible conferences which met annually after 1876. From this base, dispensationalism, as his scheme was called, found its way into most of the Protestant denominations. This development was greatly accelerated by C.I. Schofield's (1843–1921) *Reference Bible*. When Darby died, the movement continued to be shepherded by a series of dominant leaders, James Butler Stoney (1814–97), Frederick Raven (1837–1903), James Taylor Sr (1870–1953), James Taylor Jr (1896–1970). Each of these individuals extended Darby's teaching of separation from evil to avoid contamination. James Taylor Sr, by all accounts a godly man, stressed the need to 'withdraw from evil'. While 'salvation was secured by faith in Christ and His finished work alone', he asserted that 'current salvation was in the church', that is, the assembly.

Core Beliefs

Verses in the Bible that have been quoted to justify not mixing with 'worldlies' include Isaiah 52:11; Psalm 1:1; 1 Corinthians 5:11, 13; 2 Corinthians 6:14–18; and 2 Timothy 2:19–22 ('pursue righteousness, faith, love and peace, along with those who call on the Lord out of a pure heart'). Members of the Exclusive Brethren also believe:

● all the doctrines of the biblical, creedal Christianity;
● that the historic and denominational churches are in a state of total and irretrievable ruin;

- in the imminent bodily return of Jesus Christ to this earth;
- in separating from all known evil, which includes people, places and entertainment;
- that their leader is 'the elect vessel' through whom God speaks.

Recent Developments

Probably the most significant development in twentieth-century Exclusive Brethren history was James Taylor Sr's proclamation of himself as universal leader and his subsequent declaration that the movement would from that point on be under the control of one man who would be designated as 'the elect vessel'. James Taylor Jr ('Big Jim') extended his father's authoritarianism and brought the movement into disrepute by his extreme teaching and disreputable personal behaviour. He introduced the doctrine of 'separate tables', forbidding a member to sit at table with any of their own family over twelve years of age who did not break bread in the assembly. This was later extended to not eating food prepared by an unbeliever.

Under Big Jim's regime other strictures were introduced. Brethren children were not allowed to socialize with other children or take part in religious education lessons or after-school activities. In 1961 all Brethren were prohibited from going to university or college and young people had to leave their courses. Soon a ban was placed on membership of any public body, including trade unions, and all occupations which required professional validation, such as medicine or pharmacy. The power which Taylor exerted eventually brought about his downfall. He became gripped by alcohol and women and his addresses were punctuated with crudities and sexual innuendoes. After one of the meetings in Aberdeen in July 1970 he was found in bed with one of his women followers. The scandal hit the national press and resulted in the loss of about 8,000 members over the next two years.

Both before and since Taylor Jr's time several smaller Exclusive breakaway groups have been formed. Most have taken the name of their faction leaders, such as Kelly (1877) and Stuart (1885); the Glantons (1908) took their name from their place of origin in Northumberland. As in the main Taylorite group, still sometimes known as 'the Jims' in deference to his leadership, Exclusive Christian Brethren ecclesiology is connexional, in that individual assemblies accept each other's disciplinary action. In the case of the Taylorites the man of God, or overall leader, exercises authority over all the assemblies.

Current Taylorite Exclusive leaders estimate the total worldwide membership at approximately 42,000, with British membership at 15,000. Former members who have left recently put the overall total at about 27,000.

Present Practice

Since the 1970s Taylorite Exclusivism has continued in much the same vein under James Symington (1914–87), a North Dakota pig farmer, and John Hales (1922–2002), a chartered accountant who was based in Sydney, Australia. His son, Bruce David Hales, succeeded him as 'universal leader' and 'elect vessel'. In recent years still stricter separation has been called for and rules have been tightened. Members were exhorted not to live in a semi-detached house or share a common wall with another business whose owner is not in fellowship. Cats, dogs and domestic pets cannot be kept and radios, televisions, mobile phones, fax machines and computers are banned 'as instruments that will smooth the way for the imminent rise of the Man of Sin'. Failure to comply with such regulations results in the individual concerned being 'withdrawn from', which means no brother or sister will eat or speak with the offender for the set period of punishment.

As Bryan Wilson, former fellow of All Souls, Oxford, noted: 'When there is persistent wrongdoing or false teaching, the local assembly becomes concerned, and if the case cannot be resolved by rebuke, then an unrepentant individual is said to be "shut up", a term used to indicate that he is not admitted to the Brethren's meetings and, in particular, to the meeting for "breaking of bread". One who fails to repent is "withdrawn from" or "put out", and any brother who fails to dissociate himself from the unrepentant himself becomes subject to the same form of censure. Little as such measures might be appreciated by outsiders, they are well understood by those who have committed themselves to the fellowship as something unfortunate but essential to the maintenance of its purity.'

Sunday worship meetings begin with a simple 'breaking of bread service' which is held at 6 a.m. with everyone including infants partaking of the emblems of the bread and wine. On these occasions the service proceeds with thanksgivings and contributions from the brothers. Since James Taylor Jr's time men have been prohibited from wearing ties. At worship it is therefore customary for men to wear open-neck shirts. There are several other times of worship during the course of a Sunday and members usually attend a 'city service' at their nearest city in the evening. Women wear headscarves in public as a sign of submission to their husbands; they have no public role in the meetings apart from giving out the numbers of the hymns, which are sung unaccompanied. In addition there are week-night prayer meetings, Bible study gatherings and from time to time three-day Bible conferences and fellowship meetings.

Since Bruce Hales assumed the overall leadership, attempts have been made to invite back into membership some of those who either left or were put out; and there appear to have been one or two minor relaxations. However, the Exclusive Brethren remains a tight-knit and highly intensive religious organization that exercises a strong control over every aspect of the lives of its members.

13.   Falun Gong (Falun Dafa)

Origins

Falun Dafa is the movement that practises Falun Gong, but the group itself is now generally referred to as Falun Gong. It was founded by Li Hongzhi, who was born in 1951 or 1952 in north-east China. It is one of a number of *qigong* (energy cultivation) groups that emerged in China in the later 1980s. The names derive from 'fa' (the law of the universe), 'lun' (wheel), 'da' (great) and 'gong' (the practice of qigong). Falun Dafa might be translated as 'the great *dharma* of the Wheel of the Law' and Falun Gong as 'the practice of the wheel of *dharma*'.

Chinese culture and religion are both focused on issues of health and wholeness and the importance of prolonging one's life, and much of what Falun Gong is about is a variety of exercises and meditations which are designed to produce renewed energy and physical health. This in turn enables adherents to reach higher levels of spiritual awareness. Li maintains there are many levels of existence. The Falun Gong symbol is a spinning swastika, which symbolizes the universe. Falun Gong focuses on the cultivation of the virtues of truthfulness, benevolence and forbearance.

Core Beliefs

Li Hongzhi is regarded by his followers as an advanced being, a Buddha, but he is not worshipped by them and Falun Gong is not a Buddhist offshoot, although some of its beliefs and practices are similar. His two books, *Zhuan Falun* (Turning of the Law Wheel) and *Falun Gong* (Law Wheel Qigong), contain the substance of his teaching and are basic reading for new members. He has a strong belief that aliens inhabit the earth and are set on corrupting the human race. His writings describe competing teachings as corrupted and unsuitable for the present stage of history. His strongest criticism is aimed at secularists with a belief in science and materiality. By following Li's teachings the devotee is able to reach a higher realm of being.

Recent Developments

The movement has been a strong campaigner for religious freedom. On 25 April 1999, after the government renewed their clampdown on spiritual movements, 10,000 Falun Gong followers held a protest outside Communist Party headquarters in Beijing. The group was outlawed as a religious cult on 22 July and was alleged to have brainwashed its followers. Falun Gong claims that at least 5,000 of their members have been sent to labour camps. The US Congress unanimously passed resolutions that criticized the Chinese government for their action in cracking down on Falun Gong.

Today there are groups active in most Asian countries as well as in Europe and the USA, where Li himself has led a reclusive lifestyle since 1998. Falun Gong claims 100 million members worldwide, 80 million of whom live in China. By contrast the

Chinese government puts the figure at 2 million. Both figures are probably inaccurate, the latter because the government perceives Falun Gong to be a threat. Some experts in the West believe that a reasonable estimate today would be far fewer than 1 million worldwide.

Present Practice

Falun Gong is a worldwide network that is open to all. Those in Europe and the West who show particular interest are invited to a free nine-day seminar. Others are given literature at open days and Falun Dafa concerts. A large proportion of the members is reported to be elderly. John Wong and William T. Liu in their book *The Mystery of China's Falun Gong: its Rise and its Sociological Implications* (1999) interpret the movement's popularity with elderly people as stemming from its provision of what is basically health care.

14. The Family (Children of God)

Origins

The roots of the Children of God (COG) as they were originally known lie in the counter-cultural youth movement of the 1960s, which spawned groups of flower children, anti-war protesters and pot-smoking backpackers. This movement was particularly strong along the California coast, where it also birthed The Jesus People. Most of these groups had one thing in common: they were disillusioned with the materialistic nature of Western society, which they felt was oppressing the poor and the nations of the Far East, most notably Vietnam.

The founder of COG was David Brandt Berg (1919–94), who was born into a godly home. His father, Hijalmer Berg, was a Christian & Missionary Alliance pastor, his mother a radio evangelist. Berg married his first wife, Janet Miller (known in The Family as Eve), in 1943 and spent his early years as a pastor in Arizona and then travelling the USA with Fred Jordan, pioneering televangelism. During this time Jordan allowed Berg to establish a Christian commune at his 'Soul Clinic Ranch' in Texas. They parted company in 1965 and Berg moved on to work as an evangelist for the Christian & Missionary Alliance. In 1967 he transferred his allegiance to the Assemblies of God, becoming the leader of their 'Teen Challenge' at Huntingdon

Beach, California. Within a short while he separated this group from the national organization and renamed it as Light Club. Many young people were attracted by the Light Clubbers and gave up their drugs and alcohol to share in Berg's evangelical vision. In 1969 Berg had a revelation that California was about to be hit by a major earthquake. This resulted in his leading the group out of California and for eight months they wandered through the south-west in caravans. It was during this travel period that they changed their name to The Children of God.

That year was of further significance for Berg, because he became a polygamist by taking a second wife, Maria. He justified his action on the basis of various Old Testament passages that enjoined the practice of polygamy. He also professed to receive a revelation that he was the 'End Time prophet' who would play a major role in the second and final return of Jesus to this earth. A number of Berg's predictions failed to materialize. On 2 November 1973, for example, he announced that 'destruction was coming upon America that would affect the whole world due to the coming comet Kohoutek'. He continued: 'You in the US have only until January to get out of the states before some kind of disaster, destruction or judgment of God is to fall because of America's wickedness.' At a later point he prophesied that Jesus would return in 1993.

In the early 1970s Berg first settled his following back in three communities in California but was then forced to disperse them across the USA on account of opposition from anti-cult activists. He later prophesied that all life in the United States was shortly going to be destroyed and this resulted in a great exodus in which almost the entire membership dispersed into various countries including India, Australia, South America and the British Isles. By the close of 1972 COG had a membership of 2,000 living in some 40 scattered colonies.

In February 1972 Berg announced that he was Moses David, the prophet of God, and his words were 'the voice of God himself'. Soon after this he began the practice of disseminating his message to his followers by means of *Mo Letters* ('Mo' being shorthand for Moses). They eventually exceeded 2,500 in number and most were written in a ragged style and produced in a rough and ready format, sometimes with sketches and diagrams that were simplistic and crude. They covered a wide range of topics including some of Berg's most controversial edicts on love, sex and marriage. The *Mo Letters* came to be regarded as scripture. Also in 1973 Berg started what was known as 'litnessing', which was a method of witnessing by distributing COG literature in exchange for financial gifts.

At some point in the 1970s Berg visited a group of gypsies in Houston, Texas, who spent part of their time contacting the dead. As a result of this meeting Berg professed to have acquired a spirit guide by the name of Abrahim, said to be a thirteenth-century gypsy king. Following this, Berg had a long-term involvement with spiritism and the occult.

In 1976 Berg told the women members in his following to engage in what he termed 'Flirty Fishing'. This edict was based on Jesus' promise to his disciples, 'I will make you fishers of men', and Berg expected them to go into restaurants, bars and pubs and encourage men towards a commitment to Christ by wearing alluring, low-cut dresses and short skirts. They were instructed to be tactile and affectionate and, if the chemistry was right, to engage in full sexual intercourse. Berg wrote: 'What better way to show them Love than to do your best to supply their desperately hungry needs for love, fellowship, companionship, mental and spiritual communication, and physical needs such as food, clothing, shelter, affection, a tender loving kiss, a soft warm embrace, the healing touch of your loving hand, the comforting feeling of your body next to theirs… and yes, even sex if need be.' In keeping with this development, COG was reorganized as the Family of Love. From this time onward it was often referred to simply as 'The Family'.

Berg described the 'flirty' women activists as 'Hookers for Jesus' and stated in his 1979 annual report that they had witnessed in this way to over a quarter of a million souls, loved over 25,000 and won about 19,000. In 1977 membership was given as only 7,500 with 7,000 living in more than 70 colonies in different parts of the world. However, with Berg's new evangelistic methods the movement reached its zenith in the early 1980s, when its membership was estimated to have risen to about 35,000.

COG under David Berg had been a tightly run ship and in consequence there had been a number of complaints of abuse on the part of the leadership. These criticisms led to the organization being given a more democratic structure. Instead of Dad (David Berg), elders and deacons, each community was established as a self-governing entity. At this time Berg introduced 'sexual sharing', which advocated free sexual relationships among the membership. There were reports of some children being involved, but almost no cases of sexual abuse were ever proved. A number of the *Mo Letters* dealt explicitly with the new sexual edicts. For example, a 1977 letter entitled *Child Brides* stated, 'I hope young kids have plenty of sex… Why did the Lord make you able to have children at the age of 11, 12, 13 if you weren't supposed to have sex then?' Another *Mo Letter* written in 1980 was entitled *The Devil Hates Sex But God Loves It*. Despite widespread accusations of child abuse, research showed that child abuse within COG households was lower than in society in general. One, however, who did claim to be abused was one of Berg's own daughters, Linda, who disclosed in her autobiography that her father first had sex with her when she was eight.

Core Beliefs

The Family of Love's beliefs are of two kinds: basic, orthodox, evangelical beliefs which are held today and edicts laid down by Berg. Some in this latter category have been rejected or modified in recent times. Their evangelical doctrines include the following:

● The Bible is the inspired word of God, given to us by God our Creator to be a 'lamp to our feet and a light to our path'. (Psalm 119:105).

● The Trinity: 'We believe in the Unity of the Godhead, that there are three distinguishable but inseparable Persons: the Father, Son, and the Holy Spirit.'

● The Biblical account of Creation as outlined in Genesis, that it is to be accepted literally, and not figuratively.

● All men and women are sinners, and 'are absolutely unable to attain to righteousness without the saving power of Jesus Christ'.

● Salvation is for 'all persons who personally accept God's pardon for sin through Jesus Christ'. Such persons once saved 'shall be kept for ever'. This is not to be taken by believers as 'a licence for sin'.

● The baptism of the Holy Spirit is 'a baptism of love' which 'may be freely obtained by all believers who simply ask God for it' and is often given after the scriptural 'laying on of hands' of other believers.

- The present time is the period known in scripture as the 'Last Days' or the 'Time of the End' that immediately precedes the second coming of Jesus Christ.
- Seven years before Jesus' return a powerful world ruler known as the Beast or Antichrist will arise and 'confirm a covenant' [peace treaty] (Daniel 9: 27). This will plunge the world into 'unprecedented social chaos and religious persecution' known in the Bible as the great tribulation.
- The great tribulation will occur three and a half years after the peace initiative. At this point the Antichrist will declare that he alone is God and demand the worship of the entire world. Nobody 'will be legally permitted to buy or sell essential goods, except those who bear this demagogue's mark or number, the "Mark of the Beast" on their right hand or forehead'.
- The second coming will follow immediately after the great tribulation and 'all of the born-again believers' will be raptured into the air in their resurrection bodies to meet the Lord in the air.
- This is followed by the Marriage Supper of the Lamb in heaven for the raptured and the battle of Armageddon on earth for the rest. Jesus and his followers will then assume control over the entire world and establish the kingdom of God on earth for a thousand years (the Millennium). After this Satan will be destroyed, followed by the final judgment and the arrival of heaven on earth with the heavenly city, New Jerusalem, descending from above.

Beliefs specifically emanating from Berg are:
- David Berg was chosen to be a latter-day prophet.
- God's only law is love. The Ten Commandments are no

longer mandatory; the only governing principle is what is loving in any given situation.

● Deception is ethically permissible in some instances, particularly in the defence of the movement. Berg set out this practice in his 1977 *Mo Letter, In Deceivers Yet True*, in which he argued that the Lord allowed his people to deceive their enemies.

● God the Father is a white-haired man who is 'a sexy naked god in a wild orgy of the Spirit' and 'a pimp' (*Mo Letters* 286 and 520).

● The birth of Jesus resulted from a sexual union between Mary and the angel Gabriel (*Mo Letters* 1566 and 2359).

● The Holy Spirit is a sensual woman enabling individuals to experience 'spiritual orgasm' (*Mo Letters* 723 and 2115).

Recent Developments

In 1985 the structure of the organization once again reverted to a more autocratic model with David and Maria Berg organizing a central office that operated under the title 'World Services'. The Bergs appointed a National Shepherd for each country and below them were District Shepherds, Local Area Shepherds and Home Shepherds. 'Flirty Fishing' was brought to a close in 1987, partly on account of widespread adverse criticism, but also due to the spread of sexually transmitted diseases among the members. The official reason given for the change of policy was that more time needed to be given to other forms of outreach. From 1987 incest and other sexual abuse was also explicitly banned and any adult found to be having sex with a person under twenty-one was immediately expelled from membership.

When Berg died in 1994 at the age of seventy-five, the leaders produced *The Love Charter*, which sets out the responsibilities of each individual member of the group. Since Berg's death the overall leadership has been in the hands of his wife, Maria David, and her second husband, Peter Amsterdam. The Family's present organizational structure consists of boards that act as committees and oversee the main aspects of the movement, such as child care, education, teenagers, public relations and pastoral care by 'visiting shepherds'. The present worldwide membership of The Family is estimated to be 13,000 full-time members, that now include social workers and academics, and 29,000 associate members in ninety countries. In the UK The Family is currently administered from the movement's European office in Luton. Published figures for the UK in 1998 revealed 200 members, a reduction from 1,000 in the late 1960s.

Present Practice

It has clearly moved on from most of the controversial edicts laid down by Berg. A British high court judge, Lord Justice Ward, declared in 1995: 'The Family have been black, very black and they are still not white, but... I have decided to trust them to continue to bring lightness into darkness.' The Family, as the name suggests, are still strongly committed to the practice of communal living. They believe that the New Testament account of the communal lifestyle practised by the early church in Jerusalem (Acts 2:44f) is not simply history but 'an exemplary pattern and model which God intended succeeding generations of believers to follow'. The Family therefore live in communes. Typically, these consist of eight to ten adults and up to twenty-five children. When new converts join, they give all their possessions to the organization. Birth control is discouraged and tobacco, alcohol and other drugs are not permitted. All the adults in each community are required to take a share in the upbringing of the children. Sexual sharing appears to still be practised, but only by consenting adult members within each group.

The Family's British headquarters were until 2002 in the manor house at Dunton Bassett, Leicestershire, where the national leader, Gideon Scott, lived with his wife Rachel (originally Linda), some of their younger children and others. Gideon, a former public school boy and Salvation Army bandsman, joined the COG in 1975 and met his wife, also from a mainstream Christian background, within the movement. Theirs was reputed to be a more conventional Christian community and members were free to leave and the public to visit. They enjoyed good relationships with the local village community.

15.   Freemasonry

Origins

The United Grand Lodge of England (UGLE) defines
Freemasonry as 'a society of men concerned with moral and
spiritual values. Its members are taught its precepts by a series
of ritual dramas, which follow ancient forms, and use
stonemasons' customs and tools as allegorical guides.' Its origins
lie in obscurity. Most present-day masons believe it is derived
from the medieval stonemason guilds and their successors. The
term 'Freemason' is derived from freestone-masons who hewed
or built in free stone as opposed to rough stone. However, by the
seventeenth century the two terms were used interchangeably. It
is clear that masons were the elite of the labour force and had
secret signs, customs and marks.

Some believe that this explanation is insufficient and that
there are also roots in ancient science and astronomy. Certainly
some present day masonic words and symbols are derived from
the early Egyptians, although this should not be taken as an
assertion that Freemasonry began in that era. Some masonic
legend and tradition has also clearly been borrowed from the
Knights Templar, an order of military monks founded by Hugh de
Payens in 1118. The order was effectively brought to an end on 13
October 1307 by Philip IV of France, who stole their lands and

possessions and instructed the Inquisition to torture any Templars he managed to capture. Many of the fit and able knights escaped to various parts of Europe and a number settled in the more isolated regions of Scotland. It is from this point that much of masonic tradition originates and mention must be made of Rosslyn Chapel, just five miles from Edinburgh. It was built by Sir William St Clair, whose family had long roots back into Templar ancestry, took forty years to build and is adorned with Templar, Enochian and some masonic imagery. The chapel also has an external window that illustrates some form of initiation service.

The earliest record anywhere of a masonic initiation is that of John Boswell, Laird of Auchenleck, who according to the lodge minutes was initiated into the Lodge of Edinburgh on 8 June 1600. The earliest records of initiation in England include Sir Robert Moray in 1641 and five years later Elias Ashmole (1616–92), founder of the Ashmolean Museum in Oxford. The first recorded American-born mason was probably Jonathan Belcher, the governor of Massachusetts, who was initiated in 1704. Very little is known about masonry for seventy years after Ashmole's initiation. By 1717, however, there were four London lodges and on 24 June the Premier Grand Lodge of England was founded, with Anthony Sayer (d. 1742) presiding over the inaugural feast. The famous Freemasons' Hall in London was built by Thomas Sandby in 1775 and rebuilt on the same site in 1932. The new structure was dedicated to 'the Glorious Dead who fought in the Great War'. The Grand Lodge of Pennsylvania was the first American lodge to be granted a constitution.

In the century that followed the founding of the grand lodges many distinguished individuals joined the masons. Among them were Sir Robert Walpole (1676–1745), Charles Montesquieu (1689–1755), Francois Voltaire (1694–1778), Benjamin Franklin

(1706–90), Frederick the Great (1712–86), George Washington (1732–99), Franz Joseph Haydn (1732–1809), Edward Gibbon (1737–94), Edward Jenner (1749–1823), Wolfgang Amadeus Mozart (1756–91), Robert Burns (1759–96) and Andrew Jackson, 7th president of the USA (1767–1845). In more recent times masons have numbered among their ranks Joseph Smith (*see The Church of Jesus Christ of Latter-Day Saints), Charles Darwin (1809–82), Oscar Wilde (1854–1900), Sir Arthur Conan Doyle (1859–1930), Rudyard Kipling (1865–1936), C.G. Jung (1875–1961), General Douglas MacArthur (1880–1964), Geoffrey Fisher, Archbishop of Canterbury (1887–1972), J Edgar Hoover (1895–1972), Norman Vincent Peale (1898–1993), Glen Miller (1909–44) and Buzz Aldrin (b. 1930).

There are three ceremonies for admitting new members and they are in two parts. Any man who wants to become a Freemason must take the initiative and find two sponsors from within the brotherhood. He is then initiated into the first degree of 'Entered Apprentice'. This takes place in the Lodge Room, which is patterned on the design of King Solomon's temple. The ceremony begins with him removing his outer clothing and standing in only his shirt, trousers, socks and left shoe. He is then blindfolded, his shirt is loosened so that his left breast is visible and a hangman's noose is placed around his neck with rope dangling behind him. The initiate is led to the door of the temple by the Tyler, who knocks seeking to gain entry. He is asked, 'Who is there?' He gives the individual's name followed by the words 'a poor candidate in a state of darkness'. At this point the inner guard places a dagger on the man's left breast. The candidate, still blindfolded, is led to a kneeling stool, where he kneels before the Worshipful Master and the blessing of heaven is sought. Various other rituals follow which culminate in the 'solemn obligation', in which the candidate places his hand on *The Volume of the Sacred Law* that is the Bible and supports a compass point on his left breast. The words include: 'I [...], in the presence of the great architect of the universe [...], solemnly promise and swear, that I will always conceal and never reveal any part or parts, point or points of the secrets or mysteries of or belonging to Free and Accepted Masons in Masonry [...]. These several points I solemnly swear to observe, without reservation of any kind, under no less penalty, on the violation of any of them, than that of having my throat cut across, my tongue torn out by the root and buried in the sand of the sea at low water mark or a cable's length from the shore, where the tide regularly ebbs and flows twice in twenty-four hours, or the more effective punishment of being branded as a wilfully perjured individual, void of all moral worth, and totally unfit to be received into this worshipful Lodge [...] so help me, God, and keep me steadfast in this my great and solemn obligation of an Entered Apprentice Freemason.' Every new Freemason receives *The Book of Constitutions* that contains the rules of membership and the penalties that can result from infringements.

In addition to Craft Masonry (Entered Apprentice, Fellow, Master Mason) there is High Masonry, in which initiates can progress up through a further thirty degrees to the thirty-third degree of 'Grand Inspector General'. These further degrees are under the jurisdiction of the Supreme Council, whose headquarters are in London. While anyone who wants to enter 'the Craft' has to take the initiative himself, the reverse is the case in regard to Higher Masonry. Only those Master Masons who are selected by the Supreme Council are offered the chance of 'being perfected'. An even smaller percentage of those who are so chosen progress beyond the eighteenth degree of 'Knight of the Pelican and Sovereign Prince Rose Croix of Heredom'. In fact, with each higher degree the number of initiates diminishes. The degree of 'Grand Inspector General' is confined to 75 members. Strange as it may seem, it is therefore the case that even the Grand Master of all England may only be a Freemason of the third degree. Whereas in England and Wales only a few of the thirty-three degrees are conferred by special ritual, in the USA each degree has its own distinctive ritual.

Core Beliefs

The United Grand Lodge of England is categorical that 'Freemasonry is not a religion, nor is it a substitute for religion.' This said, in their lodge meetings Freemasons meet in front of an open Bible and sing and pray to God and all members are expected to have a belief in God, whether the Christian deity, Allah or the supreme being of another major world faith. Freemasonry thus professes to be a supporter of religion but does not regard itself as a religion.

- Freemasons believe in the Supreme Being as expressed by any of the major world religions. This Supreme Being is referred to as 'the great architect'.

- In Higher Masonry Jesus is seen as a merely human. In the Maundy Thursday Rose Croix service, attended by all thirty-third degree masons, the leader says: 'My brothers, we meet this day to commemorate the death of our most wise and perfect Master – NOT as inspired or divine, but as at least the greatest of all humanity.'

- In the initiation to the third or highest degree of Craft Masonry 'the great architect' is revealed as the syncretistic

deity 'Jah-Bul-On'. Jah is Yahweh, the God of the Old
Testament, Bul is Baal, a Canaanite deity whom the Israelites
were forbidden to worship and On is Osiris, the ancient
Egyptian god of the underworld.

● Freemasons believe in the importance of the Bible, which is
referred to as *The Volume of the Sacred Law* and is always open
at every Masonic meeting.

● Norman Vincent Peale, best-selling author of *The Power of
Positive Thinking* (1952), *Jesus of Nazareth* (1966) and *Power of
the Positive Factor* (1987), a Christian minister at New York
City's Marble Collegiate Reformed Church from 1932 to 1984
and a thirty-third degree mason, wrote: 'I consider Masonry
to be the purest religion on earth.'

Recent Developments

The United Grand Lodge of England clarified the basic
principles of Freemasonry in 1929. They include the prohibition
of any discussion concerning religion and politics within the
lodge. Additionally, UGLE steadfastly refuses to make any
pronouncements on matters of foreign or domestic policy,
however urgent a particular situation may appear. The Home
Grand Lodges reaffirmed this commitment in 1949.

For a local lodge to be recognized by UGLE it must be
established by a regular grand lodge or by three or more private
lodges which are recognized by a grand lodge. It must be fully
self-governing with no influence of any kind over its affairs from
any other masonic body. It must also have full control over the
symbolic degrees of Entered Apprentice, Fellow Craft and
Master Mason.

Under the Grand Lodge of England and Wales in 2002, there were 330,000 Freemasons meeting in 8,644 lodges. There are separate Grand Lodges for Scotland with 100,000 members and Ireland with 70,000. Worldwide there are an estimated 5 million members. Freemasonry is particularly strong in the United States and Canada as well as in a number of European countries, most notably France and Germany. It also played a significant role in the unification of Italy. Each state has its own grand lodge and grand chapter. The majority of British Freemasons are middle-class and many of them are members of the military, judiciary and medical professions. A number of large companies and hospitals have their own lodges. A number of the British aristocracy and gentry have been masons. Higher degree masonry is governed by supreme councils that exist in many parts of the world, including London. The senior body is the Supreme Council of Charleston, South Carolina, which exercises a powerful influence across the globe.

Present Practice

Freemasons are well known for their generosity and charitable work. They are taught to give to the needs of the local community and to major world concerns and relief and medical work. From the very beginning Freemasons have been involved in care for the sick, the orphans and the aged. Masons have been responsible for building hospitals and clinics. When a new member is initiated, he is charged with the responsibility of fulfilling his civil, public and professional duties. Freemasons are required as a condition of membership not to use 'the Craft' to promote their own businesses or personal and professional interests. Any attempt to protect a fellow Freemason who has acted unlawfully is utterly forbidden.

There is a strong sense of secrecy surrounding Freemasonry. While it is the case that masons are free to declare their membership and will do so if asked for good reason, they are not free to disclose details of internal meetings, ceremonies and practices. Ritual plays an important part in that it helps to strengthen bonds of friendship between the brotherhood. The secrets also include various ways of recognizing fellow members when away from home or visiting a lodge in another part of the country. Freemasonry is non-political and any form of political discussion at meetings is prohibited.

Freemasonry has no creed or formal beliefs and there are no sacraments. The basic lodge rituals are not concerned with salvation. At lodge meetings various business matters are attended to, including finance and correspondence. From time to time there will be the election of new officers and the annual installation of the Master. The admission of new masons (see above) is obviously another important occasion.

No mainstream lodge or grand lodge of masons accepts women as members. The reason usually given for this is that lodges were formed to be a fraternity of males and the admission of women would defeat that purpose. There are, however, some mixed lodges. The Order of the Eastern Star in the USA requires its primary officer to be female (worthy matron) with a male by her side (worthy patron). In England and Wales there are at least two grand lodges (not mainstream) that are solely for women and one that admits both men and women, the Grand Lodge Droit Humaine.

16.   Friends of the Western
                Buddhist Order

Origins

The Friends of the Western Buddhist Order (FWBO) was
founded in London in 1967 by Sangharakshita, formerly Dennis
Lingwood, who was born in London in 1925. In his childhood
years Lingwood had suffered considerable illness, with the
result that he became a prodigious reader and developed an
early love for art and culture. At sixteen he read *Diamond Sutra*
and had mystical experiences that cemented his convictions
that he was and indeed always had been a Buddhist. During the
Second World War he was conscripted to India in 1943 and he
remained there when the conflict ended. After a period of travel
he settled in the holy city of Benares (now Varanasi, Uttar
Pradesh) and undertook a period of study under Bhikkhu
Jagdish Kashyap (1908–76), a Buddhist teacher of the Theravada
tradition who was professor of Pali at the University of Benares.
Kashyap persuaded the Englishman to settle in the border town
of Kalimpong and 'work for the good of Buddhism'.

On 12 May 1949 Lingwood was ordained a Theravada
Buddhist monk and given the name Sangharakshita, meaning
'protected by the community'. A short time later the Tibetan

Buddhist lama, Dhardo Rinpoche (1917–90), gave Sangharakshita the Mahayana *bodhisattva* ordination, which commits the ordinand to saving all beings everywhere from suffering.

Kalimpong remained his place of residence until he received an invitation in the mid-1960s to go to England, part of the aim being to help with a dispute that had arisen at the Buddhist *vihara* in Hampstead. His visit was not well received by all those who had invited him, partly because there were rumours of his having entered into a sexual relationship. Nevertheless, after a brief farewell visit to India, he returned to England convinced that there was a clear need for Buddhist teaching. Having founded the FWBO in 1967, he founded the Western Buddhist Order (WBO) the following year in India. The WBO consists of those who have been ordained in public recognition of their full-time commitment; the FWBO are essentially lay members who have other jobs and pursue their Buddhist practice in a lay, part-time capacity; individuals join the WBO through first contacting the WBO and attending their courses.

Sangharakshita emphasized the basic Buddhist teachings, such as the Four Noble Truths, but disregarded teachings which he felt were not relevant to the West. He stressed the central act of becoming a Buddhist as 'going for refuge to the Buddha'. When people suffer they turn for refuge to relationships, sex, chocolate and material things. Sangharakshita taught that 'Three Jewels' are true refuge, namely the Buddha himself, the teachings or truth (*dharma*) and the Buddhist community (*sangha*). A Buddhist is thus someone who finds refuge in the Three Jewels.

Sangharakshita conceived 'going for refuge' in a series of different levels. *Ethnic* going for refuge is when one is born into a Buddhist culture. *Provisionally* going for refuge is where an individual has made a personal commitment to Buddhism. *Effective* going for refuge is where that commitment is producing Buddhist ethical behaviour. Beyond this are *real* going for refuge and *cosmic* going for refuge.

Core Beliefs

- The Four Noble Truths:
  1. **all life is suffering**
  2. **the cause of all suffering is craving**
  3. **stopping desire will stop suffering**
  4. **the Eightfold Path is the best way to stop suffering.**
- The Noble Eightfold Path:
  1. **right views**
  2. **right resolve**
  3. **right speech**
  4. **right action**
  5. **right livelihood**
  6. **right effort**
  7. **right mindfulness**
  8. **right concentration or meditation**
- Making it the goal of our existence to reach nirvana (a state of complete and serene detachment).
- Dependent arising (the belief that things arise in dependence on causes).
- Going for refuge to the Buddha, the dharma and the sangha (the Three Jewels).

Recent Developments

In the 1990s Sangharakshita began the process of handing over the responsibility for the administration and spiritual life of the movement to a group of senior men and women disciples. This process was completed by 2000 and the FWBO leadership is now in the hands of twelve men and women who are known as the College of Public Preceptors. Sangharakshita still exerts a considerable influence over the movement. FWBO has 30 centres in the UK and another 50 in other parts of the world, including India. The WBO reached 1,000 members in 2002. It is estimated that 20,000 people attend FWBO meditation courses in the UK each year.

Present Practice

The FWBO and WBO do not draw a rigid distinction between the laity and those who are monastics. Those who are in the 'effective going for refuge' category are not necessarily celibate. Nor is there any distinction made between men and women; Order members, whether *Dharmacaris* (male followers of the *dharma*) or *Dharmacarinis* (female followers of the *dharma*), are ordained on the same basis.

Sangharakshita's teaching stresses the importance of spiritual friendship (*kalyana*). Members are encouraged to spend as much time as possible with those who share the Order's ideals. Meditation is regarded as very important. It has several purposes, including mindfulness of breathing, which improves concentration, cultivation of positive thinking and loving kindness, and leads to enlightenment. Another common practice is formless meditation, where adherents simply sit and assimilate positive experiences.

Members engage in regular worship (*puja*), which consists of various prostrations, confessions, rejoicing in merit and the recitation of verses that focus on the Buddha. The FWBO and WBO are diverse movements, whose members are drawn from all classes, from academics and professionals to *avarnas* ('untouchables') in India. Many live in single sex communities and adopt a semi-monastic lifestyle, some live in traditional families; one in six is married.

17.

The International Churches of Christ

Origins

The International Churches of Christ (ICOC) has its roots in the American Churches of Christ, which emerged from American Restorationism in the later nineteenth century and finally became a denomination in its own right in 1906. Beginning with a membership of 160,000 in that year, it reached 1.2 million in the 1990s.

In 1967 the Gainesville Church of Christ in Florida embarked on an evangelistic crusade among the students of Florida University under the title 'Campus Advance'. The campaign's 'Soul Talk Bible Studies' required participants to 'open up' and share their innermost secrets, worries, fears and concerns. One of those powerfully affected by the experience was Thomas 'Kip' McKean (b. 1955), a chemistry student who was converted in 1972. After graduation in 1979 McKean took on the pastorate of the struggling Lexington Church of Christ, later called the Boston Church of Christ. Kip McKean's church expanded very rapidly and he soon developed a vision to set up 'pillar churches' in key world cities, including London, Birmingham and Sydney. In the late 1980s he officially broke with the mainline Churches of Christ.

By 1982 planters had gone out from Boston and established congregations in Chicago and New York City. By 1993 the movement had 130 congregations in different parts of the world. Much of this early growth was due to the fact that the mainline denominations, and the American Church of Christ in particular, were in a state of institutional decline. By the close of 1998 the London Church of Christ had seven zone congregations and was supporting 80 full-time leaders working in London.

Core Beliefs

ICOC beliefs are very largely in keeping with those of orthodox creedal Christianity. The key doctrinal difference is baptism.

- The ICOC assert that, for a baptism to be valid, the candidate must be 'someone who has already become a disciple'. This teaching is derived from a particular understanding of Matthew 28:19–20, in which Jesus gives the commission to 'go and make disciples, baptizing them in the name of the Father, the Son and the Holy Spirit'. This is taken to mean that a person who is being baptized must at that time be a disciple; he or she must be being discipled by another church member who is giving them input on a regular weekly basis. Bare faith or mere trust in Jesus for forgiveness is not sufficient for salvation. It is not counted for righteousness unless the candidate is being discipled and is consciously aware at the moment of baptism that they are being saved. Thus, in the words of one of their key texts, 'the new life begins in baptism'.

- The London Church of Christ published ten articles of belief, including the Bible 'in its entirety' as 'the divinely inspired word of God'; 'the church needs to continue the work of Jesus in helping the poor and needy' (Galatians 2:10).

Recent Developments

In 1986 the church put a campaign called HOPE into operation, which stood for 'Heaven's Opportunity Proclaimed Everywhere'. This was aggressive 'in your face' evangelism that included 'restauranting', 'tubing' and 'busing'; that is, small groups of church members would buttonhole members of the public wherever the opportunity arose, engaging them in conversation and distributing leaflets and invitations to services. More nerve-racking was 'halling', which involved standing up at the end of a classical concert and inviting the audience to church. Since the later 1990s ICOC's evangelism has become much less intensive, with the emphasis on inviting neighbours to meetings and social occasions.

In the autumn of 2001 McKean took a year's sabbatical 'to deal with family concerns'. Following this he stood down in November 2002 as head of ICOC because of his own rule that church leaders must resign if their children leave the church. This occurred in his own case when his daughter, who was studying at Harvard University, left the Boston International Church of Christ. McKean's resignation brought many hurts and widespread grievances into the open. Leaders were criticized for their large homes, high salaries and opulent living. It was acknowledged that there had been unnecessary team-building occasions that included 'Hawaiian retreats, deep-sea fishing expeditions and business-class tickets'. The church publicly acknowledged that its top-down management style was excessively abusive and had produced 'a culture of oppression' based on personal discipling. It had not respected human dignity and had practised 'coercive giving'.

Following McKean's resignation ICOC has endeavoured to dismantle its authoritarian leadership structure. In the new system, instead of one person acting as head over the church's nine world sector leaders, each sector is now led by a small group.

In April 1991 there were 340 International Churches of Christ worldwide with a total average Sunday attendance of 179,732. By 2002 this figure had risen to 440 congregations with an average attendance of 196,651. By 2003, however, the figure had fallen to 135,000 worldwide. Giving also declined steeply in 2003–04, although there are now some signs of recovery.

Present Practice

Since 2003 evangelism continues to be a high priority, with the main aim of interesting people in an informal Bible study session. ICOC's controversial top-down, authoritarian structure has been replaced with small sector teams. Part of discipleship (based on Hebrews 13:17) is to submit to leaders even if you believe them to be wrong. This is justified on the ground that even Jesus submitted himself to authority that was both wrong and abusive. Additionally, every member is expected to be discipled by a more spiritually mature Christian with authority to teach him or her to 'obey everything that Jesus commanded' (Matthew 28:20). Since the upheavals of 2003 discipleship, while still regarded as important, particularly in the case of younger members, is now much less intensive. 'Opening up your struggles' (to share your worries) is seen as an integral aspect of this process, although it is now encouraged, not forced.

In general ICOC members are highly committed in terms of their time and financial giving. Some members only have one free night a week. All are expected, but no longer pressurized, to tithe (give a tenth of their income) and once a year disciples are required to give fourteen to sixteen times their normal weekly tithe to help evangelize the poorer countries in the developing world. Most save during the course of the year for this. Baptism is still seen as essential to salvation, but the emphasis is more on repentance than discipleship. The ICOC is a vigorous conversionist movement that is making marked inroads among the young and students in some of the world's major cities, including those traditionally regarded as closed to Christianity.

18.   ISKCON: The International Society for Krishna Consciousness

Origins

Although the International Society for Krishna Consciousness (ISKCON), most often referred to as Hare Krishna, was only established in the sixth decade of the twentieth century, its roots are found in Hindu scripture and most notably the *Bhagavad Gita*. Orthodox Hindus worship Vishnu as the supreme deity and regard Krishna as merely an incarnation (*avatar*) of him. ISKCON regards Krishna as the supreme deity, all-powerful, all-knowing and eternal. The *Bhagavad Gita* emphasizes the importance of loving devotion to the god Krishna. With the passing of time this knowledge was almost completely lost until the early sixteenth century, when a major revival took place in India under Sri Caitanya Mahaprabu (c. 1486–1533), sometimes known as Gouranga, who is still revered by many as an *avatar* of God himself.

Sri Caitanya, who gained a huge following in India, taught the importance of Krishna consciousness. He stressed that the easiest means to attain this deep awareness was by chanting

God's holy names: 'Hare Krishna, Hare Krishna, Krishna, Krishna, Hare Hare, Hare Rama, Hare Rama, Rama, Rama, Hare, Hare'. Sri Caitanya broke with traditional custom and welcomed the participation of low-caste persons and non-Hindus.

It was His Divine Grace A.C. Bhaktivedanta Swami Prabhupada (1896–1977) who brought the teachings of Sri Caitanya to the Western world. Swami Prabhupada was born in Calcutta and studied Philosophy, English and Economics at Calcutta University. In 1922 he met Siddhartha Goswami, who instructed him in Krishna consciousness and requested him to broadcast his knowledge in English. Swami Prabhupada remained in his home town until 1950, where he worked part-time in the pharmaceutical industry in order to fund his studies and writing. In that year he withdrew from society altogether to pursue his religious vision. He left his wife and five children and lived a secluded life in the historic temple of Radha-Damodara in the city of Vrndana. He became a *sannyasin* (a Hindu ascetic). His followers used to say that 'he retired from family life'. He did not opt out of his financial responsibilities and in his final will he left generous funding for his wife and children from royalty monies.

In 1965 Prabhupada set out from his homeland for the USA. He arrived in New York City wearing his robe and sandals and begging bowl but little else. He quickly won adherents among the hippies of the Bowery district and the following year, in July 1966, he established Krishna worship in a disused store that had formerly been known as 'Matchless Gifts'. The movement's objective is to promote 'spiritual enlightenment' and to spread the pure love of Krishna throughout the world. The first outdoor session of chanting was held in Tompkins Square Park. Others soon followed.

Prabhupada's newly formed organization quickly spread to

San Francisco and a number of other American cities. Sociologists have been quick to point out that this movement took root in the heyday of youth counter-culture. Large numbers of the early members in the USA were hippies and backpacking teenagers. Krishna was a very appealing figure to the kids of the 1960s. He was youthful, happy, played the flute and chilled out with pretty girls.

Within a decade the International Society for Krishna Consciousness (ISKCON) grew into a worldwide confederation with more than a hundred temples. According to Prabhupada the Hindu equivalent of the soul (*atman*) is like a light burning deep within, but buried and covered by accumulated dirt which has resulted from a lifetime of self-gratification focused on materialism, power and prestige. This residue can be dispersed by renouncing the world, meditating and chanting and so filling one's life with the power and presence of Krishna. Initiated members of ISKCON chant the Lord's name for a minimum of one to one and a half hours each day as a regular meditation. This consists of sixteen rounds of the Hare Krishna mantra on a string of 108 prayer beads. Individual personal chanting is called *japa* meditation; where done in groups it is *kirtan* chanting.

Core Beliefs

● The one true god, Brahma, the creator, has many manifestations, including animals and fish as well as human manifestations or incarnations. The most important manifestations of Brahma are Rama, Shiva and Krishna.

● Krishna is more than the supreme manifestation of God. He is the fullness of God. Krishna is THE Godhead. Krishna has supreme power. Krishna is 'alive in the heart of every living entity'.

● Krishna can be known in a loving, personal way.
● Only Krishna-conscious beings will experience the realm of ultimate and eternal bliss.
● Salvation is progressive and based on karma. The goal is to break away from endless, repetitive reincarnations (*samsara*).
● Daily chanting of *mahamantra* (*maha* meaning great, *mantra* chant), which is: 'Hare Krishna, Hare Krishna, Krishna, Krishna, Hare Hare, Hare Rama, Hare Rama, Rama, Rama, Hare, Hare'. These sixteen words are said 108 times using the *japa mala*, a big rosary of 108 beads. This chanting has a purifying and cathartic impact. In Prabhupada's own words, 'It cleanses one's heart from all material dirt.' It also 'cleanses the accumulated dust of past karma from the mind'.

Recent Developments

In 1968 Prabhupada started an experimental farming community in the hills of West Virginia, known as Vrndavana. In the same year six American ISKCON members came to Britain. The following year the Beatles' guitarist George Harrison gave considerable impetus to the movement by recording the song, 'My Sweet Lord', based on the Hare Krishna chant. It sold 70,000 copies on the first day and eventually reached number 12 in the charts.

In 1972 Prabhupada began to invest in educational enterprises, with the founding of the Gurukula School in Texas. This institution was not simply an ISKCON school but offered a complete education. In the same year the Bhaktivedanta Book Trust (BBT) was formally established to publish and market the writings of Prabhupada and India's spiritual classics. The Book Trust is based at Croome House in Watford, England, a large manor house with seventeen acres of woods and gardens given to ISKCON in 1973 by a generous benefactor. This has proved to be a valuable centre for worship and residential conferences. The Society now has about 300 practising, ordained members in Britain and over 12,500 supporting lay members who live at home and hold secular employment; there are also major Hare Krishna temples at Letchmore Heath, at Soho Street in London and in other cities including Birmingham, Manchester and Newcastle.

Worldwide there are 300 temples, 40 rural communities and 80 restaurants in 71 countries. Hare Krishna is strongest in India and the USA, where there are over 50 temples and rural centres. There are nine centres in Australia and others in Africa and Latin America. The present headquarters of the movement are in Los Angeles, where the movement's magazine *Back to Godhead* is published. The emphasis at present seems to be on conferences, weekend retreats and the publication of literature through the Bhaktivedanta Book Trust.

Present Practice

There are three successive stages to achieve Krishna Consciousness: the Trial Stage lasts for six months; in the Initiation Stage (*Hari-Nama*) devotees are given a new name; in stage three, the Brahminical Initiation, each person receives a sacred thread and a secret mantra (*gayatri*). Initiated members must keep four basic rules of conduct: no gambling; no intoxicants, which includes all narcotics, alcoholic beverages, tobacco and coffee (narcotics may only be used for medical purposes); no illicit sexual relations (sexual relations are only allowed between individuals married by a qualified devotee; sex being increasingly regarded as for procreation only); and no violence, which leads to a strict vegetarian diet that includes abstention from fish or eggs. All initiated temple members must wear simple, distinctive clothing. For men this is a shirt (*khirtan*) and loin cloth (*dhoti*) which wraps between the legs. Women must wear a sari, which is designed to hide bodily form and so play down physical attraction. Whether in the temple or elsewhere, sleep is limited to six hours a night. Cleanliness is very important. Every time devotees come in off the street they are required to shower. Initiated members must shower after defecating. They must not use toilet paper.

The main scripture used by ISKCON members is Prabhupada's translation of the *Bhagavad Gita*. This is read as literal history rather than a symbol or poetry. Lay members are encouraged to set up an altar in their homes on a mantelpiece or corner table. The essentials are a picture of Sri Prabhupada, a picture of Sri Caitanya and his associates and a picture of Radha and Krishna. In addition, an altar cloth, water cups (one for each picture), a special plate for offering food, candles with holders and fresh flowers are recommended. Full-time temple members often have a demanding schedule, which includes *sankirtana* chanting and singing in the street. This represents a form of preaching and a declaration of Krishna's presence in a neighbourhood. While some initiates dance and chant, others spend their time fundraising by selling *Back to Godhead* magazines. Money earned in this way is called *laksmi*, Laksmi being the Hindu goddess of fortune. All initiated men are required to shave their heads except for a pigtail (*sikha*), which indicates their membership. In the past it was quite common to see ISKCON men clad in long robes and sporting their pigtails while dancing. At present such individuals are more likely to put on suits and wear a wig, as this facilitates contact with passers-by. A typical day for a temple member begins at 4 a.m. with rising and showering and several services and a devotional period before breakfast at 9 a.m. This is followed by preaching and selling literature in teams, with more of the same after lunch until about 5 p.m. Following supper adherents retire to bed.

During his lifetime Prabhupada succeeded in holding together what had become a global movement. His principal publications were word-for-word translations and commentaries on the *Bhagavad Gita*, the *Bhagavata Purana* and the *Caitanya-Caritamrita*, which is an account of the life and teachings of Caitanya Mahaprabu. When Prabhupada died in 1977, the ISKCON world was divided into eleven administrative zones, each presided over by a guru. These leaders, known as the Governing Body Council, were *sanyassins*, required by Prabhupada always to be thinking of Krishna. In the first decade of Governing Body rule there was considerable tension between the various regions and their leaders and there were accusations of sexual licence and sustained sexual abuse of children, gun arsenals and disagreements which were alleged to have resulted in killings. There were also reports that some temple officials lived in luxurious accommodation and enjoyed opulent lifestyles.

In the 1980s, in particular, women appeared to be regarded as inferior in many ISKCON temples. However, by the later 1990s a number of women were temple presidents.

19.   The Jehovah's Witnesses

Origins

The early development of the Jehovah's Witnesses is closely linked with the life and teaching of the first four leaders and presidents of the movement. The first of these, Charles Taze Russell (1852–1916), was the son of a Pennsylvania draper. Born in the town of Allegheny, he entered into partnership with his father and managed a chain of clothing stores. Russell reacted against the Congregational Church, of which he was a member, but was brought back to faith in Christ in 1868 as a result of a sermon on the second coming by Jonas Wendell, the author of a book entitled *Present Truth*, in which he asserted that Christ would return in 1873. Excited by what he had heard, Russell developed a deep interest in Adventism and began to gather a study group around him in Pittsburgh. Russell's circle differed strongly from the Adventists in one important respect: Jesus' second coming would be spiritual and invisible rather than physical.

In 1879 Russell established his own journal under the title *Zion's Watchtower and Herald of Christ's Presence*. This swiftly led to the formation of other congregations all over the USA. In 1881 he constituted his following as Zion's Watchtower Tract Society with himself as manager. As a major part of this strategy Russell began what subsequently turned into a seven-volume work, later entitled *Studies in the Scriptures*. In 1879 Russell married Marie Frances Ackerly, a well-educated woman who had been one of his Bible students. They divorced in 1913, according to Mrs Russell, on account of his 'domination and improper conduct in relation to women'. However, little evidence of immorality or cruelty was brought to light.

As the Campbellites, Millerites and Adventists and others had done, Russell predicted the date of Christ's return. His first date of 1874 failed to materialize and was advanced to 1878. Disappointment inevitably followed and Russell began to teach that Jesus had in fact returned in 1874, but invisibly, and the elect would be taken to heaven in 1914.

Russell's successors in the leadership of the movement each made a significant contribution. Joseph Franklin Rutherford (1869–1942), who succeeded Russell in 1916, had been the movement's legal officer. For a brief period he served as a substitute judge, which caused him to be known in the movement as 'Judge' Rutherford. He was a fertile author who, despite a punishing schedule of travel and speaking engagements, averaged a book a year. In 1920 he published his most celebrated volume, *Millions Now Living Will Never Die*. Rutherford moved away from 1874 and even 1914 and maintained that 1925 was the time when the rule of God would be established on earth.

Rutherford made sure the movement would be under much tighter control than formerly. In 1922 he took the step of requiring the *Watchtower* magazine to be studied in congregational groups as well as individually. As an aid to members, questions to be discussed were also printed. To the present time the *Watchtower* carries the text for Sunday Bible study in Kingdom Halls (as their meeting places are known) throughout the world. It was also during Rutherford's presidency, in 1931, that the name 'Jehovah's Witnesses' was first adopted.

Rutherford was succeeded by Nathan Knorr (1905–77). Under his presidency a number of significant doctrinal books were produced including *Let God Be True* (1946), which ran to more than 17 million copies. In 1961 *The New World Translation of the Bible* was published, which is used by all Jehovah's Witnesses, other versions being regarded as secondary. A major blow during Knorr's presidency was the failure of the prediction, in the 8 October 1966 issue of *Awake*, that the world would end in 1975. The organization acknowledged their error in the *Watchtower* of 15 March 1980.

Core Beliefs

- Witnesses believe in one God, whom they call 'Jehovah'. They reject the doctrine of the Trinity, seeing Jesus as 'a mighty one but not almighty as Jehovah God is'.
- Jesus is seen as 'the first of Jehovah God's creations' (Colossians 1:15).
- The Holy Spirit is not regarded as a person but rather as 'God's active force' that enables God's people to live for him.
- The great future hope to which all Witnesses look forward will only be realized after the cataclysmic end-time battle known as Armageddon. At the conclusion of this conflict, faithful witnesses will enjoy God's promised salvation.
- There will be two categories of the saved, the 'little flock' or 144,000 and the 'great company' or other sheep to whom Jesus referred in John 10:16.

Recent Developments

Witnesses are under the direction of their governing body, which consists of twelve men and a president. It is regarded as a theocracy or the means through which Jehovah God carries out his kingdom work on earth. They decide all matters of doctrine and public policy. They also have oversight of all writing, including books, tracts and, above all the *Watchtower*, which prints the Bible studies which every congregation throughout the world must follow at their Sunday meetings. Jehovah's Witnesses currently work in more than 230 countries. These are arranged in branches which are directly accountable to the governing body. Only those who feel they are part of the 'little flock' are permitted to take the bread and wine at the annual Memorial Communion which is celebrated on 14 Nisan. In 2002 some 8,760 partook of the sacrament out of a total worldwide attendance of 15,597,746. In 2003 it was 8,565 out of 16,097,622.

Present Practice

The more committed Witnesses spend whatever time they can going from door to door, seeking to share their faith and distribute the *Watchtower*. For many this is about ten hours a month. They are called 'publishers' and numbered 6,350,564 in 2000. In addition there are 'pioneers' who are able to make a greater commitment and may spend as much as fifty hours a month 'sharing' their faith. There are other adherents who worship at Kingdom Halls and attend the annual Memorial service. Jehovah's Witnesses are known for their rejection of blood transfusions. What is less well known is their high stress on the importance of family life and discipline. They do not bear arms, stand aloof from politics and take no part in elections. They do not celebrate birthdays, the festivals of Christmas and Easter, or New Year's Day, May Day and Mother's Day because of their possible association with pagan gods.

20.   The Jesus Movement

Origins

The Jesus Movement was a young Christian response in the 1960s and 1970s to the hippie movement. Its origin and primary location were on the west coast of the USA from where it impacted other areas of the world including the UK and parts of Europe. A number of accounts date its beginning from the opening by Ted and Elizabeth Wise and some of their friends of a small coffee house ministry, The Living Room, in San Francisco's Haight-Ashbury district. It lasted for two years and was estimated to have made contact with thirty to fifty thousand young people. What subsequently spread out from this small beginning was in many ways a counter-cultural movement. Many of the so-called 'baby boomers' who were born in the unexpected birth-rate surge between 1945 and 1960 were disenchanted with materialism and warmongering governments and threw in their lot with the hippies, while others became 'Jesus Freaks'. This name was originally pejorative but adopted because many of those who gave their lives to Christ retained a hippie style while adopting strong biblical ethics and values.

'Jesus People' were known for their openness and honesty. They were also deeply concerned about justice and environmental issues. In theological terms they were strongly fundamentalist with a firm belief in the miraculous, signs and wonders and demonic possession. Most reacted against materialism and many sought to counteract it by living rough or joining communities. The term 'Jesus Freak' aptly described their Jesus-centredness and their great enthusiasm and zeal to evangelize. They placed a strong emphasis on visions, prophecies and the end times, and many were possessed with a strong sense that Jesus' return to earth was imminent. Lonnie Frisbee, a leading Jesus Freak, suggested that the Six Day War of June 1967 between Israel and the surrounding Arab nations had set the stage for the last days before Christ's second coming. He also noted that the Old Testament book of Joel prophesied that a great outpouring of the Holy Spirit, the fulfilment of which he took to be the Jesus People, would precede the earthly return of Christ. The mood of the time resonated in a captivating song by the foremost Christian rock musician, Larry Norman (b. 1947). Entitled 'I Wish We'd All Been Ready', it describes the return of Christ and the subsequent rapture, for which many would be unprepared, due to all the wars, poverty and other evils that exist in our world.

Two books that were widely read by those within the movement were Hal Lindsey's *The Late Great Planet Earth* (1970) and Ronald Sider's *Rich Christians in an Age of Hunger* (1977). John and Elizabeth Sherrill's book *They Speak with Other Tongues* (1964) added a strong charismatic dimension. In contrast to the established churches, which were regarded as a 'dead letter', Jesus People engaged in worship which was free and spontaneous. Praise was expressed with uplifted hands with simple declarations of 'Praise the Lord', 'Thank you, Jesus' and 'Hallelujah'. In street speak Jesus was 'cool' and the Holy Spirit experience was 'far off'. Coffee houses, sometimes offering free doughnuts, became a frequent part of the scene. Their walls were often covered with banners and posters that advertised 'Under New Management' and 'Have a Nice Forever'.

The Jesus Movement began in the San Francisco area, but it soon extended to other US cities, most notably Los Angeles, Seattle, New York and Chicago. From there its teaching and lifestyles found a way to Europe and the UK. There was no overall leader; rather there were charismatic individuals who formed their own organizations. Some of these were communal, others focused on a church building, albeit an untraditional one.

Among the more prominent leaders was a former art student, Lonnie Frisbee (1950–93). Initially he had been a member of the first commune at Novato, California. He had then followed what seemed to be God's call and hitchhiked to southern California. Here he met Chuck Smith (b. 1927), who was to be another prominent figure in the early stages of the movement. In 1965 Smith had become pastor of the twenty-five-member congregation at Calvary Chapel in Costa Mesa. Smith recruited Frisbee and his wife Connie to work with the youth. Together they set up a commune called The House of Miracles. Frisbee proved a star attraction, spending his days evangelizing hippies in local parks and on the beachfronts. Within two years Calvary Chapel was filled to overflowing with more than 2,000 converts who were captivated by the nightly services and Frisbee's full-blooded Pentecostal approach, which included 'signs and wonders', that is people being healed, seeing visions, finding remarkable guidance and provision of money and resources. At these meetings people were often said to have 'been slain in the spirit' because they fell to the ground overcome with what they took to be the sense of God's presence and love.

There was constant tension between Smith and Frisbee over these spiritual manifestations and after only four years Frisbee moved on. Although his marriage broke up in 1973, he subsequently had a profound effect on John Wimber's Vineyard movement and travelled with Vineyard teams throughout the world for over three years. He died of Aids in 1993. John Wimber (1934–97) founded and directed the Association of Vineyard Churches, which grew to approximately 450 congregations within the USA with 250 more in other countries. Vineyard churches emphasize healings and other charismatic gifts, including exorcism and prophecy.

Other prominent figures in the movement included Arthur Blessitt (b. 1940), Larry Norman, Linda Meissner, Jim and Sue Palosaari, David Berg (*see The Family) and Dave Wilkerson (b. 1931). Arthur Blessitt came into the public eye after preaching at a strip club and as the minister of Sunset Strip, where he founded *His Place,* a cleaner type of nightclub, in 1965. The Sheriff's department, prompted by local vice lords and business people who feared the influence of Blessitt's 'born again' clubbers, eventually drove his clientele away by strict enforcement of the loitering laws. After a spell attempting to do something similar in New York, Blessitt opted for a cross-dragging ministry. Having successfully taken the cross from shore to shore, he felt the call of God to go overseas.

Linda Meissner was brought up on a farm in rural Iowa and attended a 'modernist' Methodist church. After several spells overseas she started to preach in Seattle, Washington, where she soon began to bring many to Christ and reported 'massive numbers receive the baptism of the Holy Spirit'. In 1969 she founded the Corps of the Jesus People's Army that for some months made a huge impact on the city's younger generation.

However, a handful of her co-leaders began to challenge her authority, which led to her to join David Berg's Children of God. Only a few of her soldiers followed her into Berg's organization, which she subsequently left.

Another locality that had strong links with the Jesus Movement was Milwaukee. Here after a brief spell in Meissner's Army Jim Palosaari and his wife Sue opened a commune named The Jesus Christ Power House. After reaching about two hundred, the membership split into four groups. Palosaari's group settled in England for a time where they were the inspiration for the *Lonesome Stone* rock musical and founded the annual Greenbelt Festival. David Wilkerson's 'Teen Challenge' and his famous work among New York's drug addicts must be accorded a place on the fringes of the Jesus Movement, as a number of his methods and techniques were later utilized by Jesus People. Wilkerson's 'Teen Challenge' was able to effect a 60 to 80 per cent cure rate for heroin addicts at a time when 5 per cent was the norm.

There were many other names and organizations that are generally seen as part of the Jesus Movement. They include Paul Wierwille's Way International, Ken Gulliksen's Bible Studies, which led on to the founding of the Vineyard churches, and the impact of musicians such as Larry Norman and Pat Boone. Among the more radical groups that the movement embraced were Tony and Susan Alamo's Christian Foundation and David Berg's Children of God. The latter organization received harsh publicity on account of Berg's use of profanities in his writings and his request to his female members to evangelize by offering sexual services.

Core Beliefs

In general terms most of the Jesus Movement's organizations held strongly Pentecostal but orthodox, biblical, creedal beliefs. The following teachings were particularly emphasized:

- the imminent bodily return of Jesus.
- the reality and danger of hell.
- the importance of the New Birth; that is, a conscious internal awareness of God's power and presence.
- the Pentecostal experience of 'baptism in the Spirit', which is an overwhelming sense of God's presence usually accompanied by speaking in tongues, an inarticulate love or prayer language.
- signs and wonders, particularly healing and exorcism.

Recent Developments and Present Practice

It is difficult to be precise as to the numbers of young people who were impacted in the 1960s and 70s. Dave Wilkerson's figure of 300,000 is generally regarded as too high. Undoubtedly there were losses and tragedies, such as the Children of God. Large numbers of the communes closed down as their organizers ran out of steam and the former radicals got married and had families. Many of the Jesus People were known to have gone later to college and universities. There have also been many enduring positives, among them the ministries of Dave Wilkerson in New York and Chuck Smith's Calvary Chapel at Costa Mesa. In total 850 Calvary Chapels were erected, 700 of them in the USA.

21.   The Nation of Islam

Origins

The Nation of Islam, which is also known as the World Community of Al-Islam in the West, the American Muslim Mission, the Nation of Peace, the Black Muslim Movement and NOI, was founded in 1930 by Wallace Dodd Ford (1877–1934), who later took the Arabic title *'Fard'* (righteousness) and the name Muhammad to signify his conversion to Islam. The details of Fard Muhammad's birthplace and early years are shrouded in obscurity. However, at some point in 1929 he left California, where he had served a prison sentence, joined the great migration to the north and settled in Detroit. In this period of great depression he began work as a door-to-door salesman selling rugs.

At this time many black Americans lived in conditions of deprivation and poverty and in consequence black nationalism flourished. Fard was particularly impressed by the teachings of the Moorish Science Temple, which Timothy Drew (later Noble Drew Ali), founded in 1913, and by the Universal Negro Improvement Association that Marcus Garvey founded in 1914. Drew Ali asserted that it was Islam rather than Christianity that was the true heritage of African peoples, so this should be embraced. He was also insistent that blacks should be regarded as superior to white people. When Drew Ali died in somewhat obscure circumstances in 1929, Fard Muhammad claimed to be his reincarnation.

Fard Muhammad developed Drew Ali's teaching and preached that Christianity was the religion of the white oppressor and that it would never free blacks from their oppression and economic disadvantages. He gradually introduced his hearers, many of whom were from Christian backgrounds, to Islamic concepts. In particular he taught that Allah is God, the white man is the devil and negroes (as blacks were commonly known at that time) are the superior race. His gospel proved popular and between 1930 and 1934 he succeeded in recruiting 8,000 followers.

When Fard Muhammad died in 1934, his right-hand man, Elijah Muhammad (1898–1975), formerly Elijah Poole, took on the leadership and established a second temple in Chicago which became the movement's headquarters. He was a dominant leader and succeeded in keeping control over the movement even during a prison sentence he served during the Second World War for avoiding the draft. During his leadership NOI's doctrines of black superiority and racial segregation solidified. He taught that the first representatives of the human race were a black people. This group, whom the NOI term 'the Original Man', created white people in a genetic experiment 6,000 years ago. Elijah Muhammad asserted that they would rule the world for 6,000 years and be destroyed at the end of this time by the blacks. Like Fard Muhammad before him, he taught that 'Islam is the original and natural religion of the Black Nation.'

During Elijah Muhammad's tenure of office, Malcolm X (1925–65), formerly Malcolm Little, became influential in the movement. The son of Louise and Earl Little of Omaha,

Nebraska, Malcolm was unable to complete his high school education and soon found himself in a world of crime and violence. In 1946 he received a seven-year prison sentence for robbery and during that time he became a committed member of the Nation of Islam. On his release he changed his name to X, a common practice among NOI members, indicating that the true tribal name of their African ancestors was unknown. Malcolm X was a powerful speaker and his public addresses brought about a dramatic rise in membership during the 1960s. Tensions with Elijah Muhammad eventually resulted in his leaving to found the Muslim Mosque Incorporated. He was assassinated in February 1965 while speaking at a meeting in Manhattan.

When Elijah Muhammad died in 1975, the leadership passed to his son, Warith Deen Muhammad (formerly Wallace Muhammad, b. 1933). His relationship with his father had been one of uneasy tension but Fard Muhammad had earlier prophesied that he would take the reins. Warith introduced a series of radical changes, which resulted in the movement adopting many traditional Islamic beliefs. A series of name changes took place, each reflecting further moves in the direction of Islamic orthodoxy. The movement was renamed the American Muslim Mission, which led to a split.

Core Beliefs

Followers of the Nation of Islam accept most of the fundamental tenets of Islam and believe:
● that there is no God but Allah, and Muhammad is his Prophet;

● that the Qur'an is the supreme scripture;
● in the Five Pillars, namely confession of faith (*shahada*) by
  reciting the creed, 'There is no God but God and Muhammad
  is his prophet'; ritual prayer (*salah*) performed five times a
  day facing Mecca; almsgiving (*zakah*); fasting (*sawm*); and
  pilgrimage to Mecca (*hajj*).

Followers of the Nation of Islam differ from the teachings of
orthodox Islam on a number of points and believe:
● Allah appeared in the flesh as Fard Muhammad (formerly
  Wallace Ford);
● there are other divine revelations after the Qur'an;
● Elijah Muhammad was a messenger in the same way as the
  Prophet Muhammad.

Recent Developments

In 1977 the NOI split into two factions, the main body continuing
to be led by Warith Deen Muhammad and the breakaway group
led by the charismatic Louis Farrakhan (b. 1933). Farrakhan had
been attracted into the movement in Boston while Malcolm X
was establishing a temple in that city. He came to resent the ways
in which Warith Deen Muhammad was altering the NOI's
beliefs and therefore left to re-establish Elijah Muhammad's
teachings as the Original Nation of Islam.

In the UK, where the exclusion order placed on Farrakhan by
the Home Secretary in 1986 was revoked in 2001, there has been a
steady growth in membership. The first study group was
established in 1989 at Brixton in south London, headed by Hilary
Muhammad, and others soon followed at Shepherds Bush and

Tottenham. The NOI has schools in Brixton, Shepherds Bush and Hackney. It is estimated that the Nation of Islam (as the two groups are known collectively) currently has between 25,000 and 100,000 adherents in the USA, Canada and Britain. In Britain there are an estimated 10,000 members, supporters and sympathizers.

Present Practice

Although NOI members worship Allah in a personal way and are encouraged to believe the truth 'in their hearts', they are expected to pray each day, in the morning, at noon, mid-afternoon, sundown and before bed. As is the custom of orthodox Muslims, they are required to pray facing Mecca. They must also attend temple worship on at least two occasions during the week. Black Muslims also have a number of dietary restrictions. These include foods such as pork and corn bread, which are regarded as unclean as well as being part of blacks' diet during their centuries of slavery in the USA. As was demonstrated by the 1995 'Million Man March' organized by Louis Farrakhan, members of the NOI have a high view of the family, which they regard as the backbone of society. Women are respected and dress modestly. Everyone is exhorted to healthy eating. Alcohol, smoking and all forms of substance abuse are banned. Gambling is forbidden.

There is considerable tension with the leaders of official Islam, who do not regard the NOI as orthodox. However, in February 2000 reconciliation took place between Louis Farrakhan and Warith Deen Muhammad and their two opposing groups, with Farrakhan promising to eschew violence and hatred. The NOI now claims to promote racial equality.

22.   The New Kadampa Tradition (NKT)

Origins

Kadampa is the Mahayana school of Buddhism that was founded by an Indian Buddhist, Master Atisha (982–1054). *Ka* means word and *dam* presentation. Kadampa is therefore Atisha's presentation of the Buddha's teachings on enlightenment that is often known as *Lamrin* or 'Lamp of the Path'.

Kadampa Buddhism was developed in the teachings of Tsongkhapa (1357–1419). Contemporary Kadampa Buddhism is called 'new' because it was first introduced into Western society in 1976 by Venerable Geshe Kelsang Gyatso (b. 1931), a Tibetan lama (priest), who has written widely on Buddhist topics. The name New Kadampa Tradition (or NKT) was finally adopted in 1991.

Gyatso has sought to make Buddhist meditation and teaching more readily accessible to twenty-first century living. An important aspect of Kadampa meditation is purifying the mind of hindrances. Once this is done, the devotees take up a concentrated focus on a particular subject, such as compassion or gentleness, and retain that focus until they feel within themselves the compassion or gentleness. Then follows the important final aspect of the meditation, which is the requirement to go and practise compassion, gentleness or whatever was the subject of the meditation. Kadampa Buddhists rely on Dorje Shugden, an emanation of the Buddha whose function is to protect them from obstacles which might prevent them from achieving their spiritual goals.

Core Beliefs

Apart from the belief that Dorje Shugden guides and protects his devotees, blesses them and increases their wisdom, the NKT core beliefs are essentially those of mainstream Buddhism:

- the law of karma, according to which bad actions or attitudes result in bad consequences;
- the power of meditation to purify negative karma and accumulate meritorious energy;
- the ability of meditation to cultivate peace and well-being and eradicate negative thought patterns.

Recent Developments

Kelsang Gyatso visited the Manjushri Buddhist Centre at Conishead Priory near Ulverston, Cumbria, England, in 1976 and this was the beginning of the New Kadampa Tradition in the West. In 1998 the first NKT temple was completed at the centre. A second temple was completed at Glen Spey in New York State and others are scheduled to follow, with the ultimate aim of establishing a temple in every major city in the world. Kadampa Buddhism has a particular appeal to Westerners and in 1996 was reported as 'Britain's biggest, richest and fastest-growing religious sect'. There are currently more than 400 Kadampa Buddhist centres in 36 countries around the world that are open to the public and where people of all cultures can learn meditation and other practices. Current membership is estimated at 5,000.

Present Practice

Adherents seek to gain wisdom by listening, contemplating and meditating. They meet together on a regular basis in a spiritual family or community (*sangha*). Within each *sangha* there are celibate monks or nuns who assist with teaching. In the USA, Europe and the British Isles there are annual meditation festivals. The majority of Kadampa Buddhists, monks, nuns, teachers and practitioners live in the Western world. Every year Kadampa festivals are held in different countries in order that Westerners can hear teachings by Venerable Geshe Kelsang Gyatso and other distinguished Buddhist teachers.

23.   Oneness Pentecostalism

Origins

Oneness Pentecostalism emerged from the wider Pentecostalism movement that began in the early 1890s. It took its origin from a revival meeting that was held at Los Angeles on 15 April 1913. At the close of the meeting Robert E. McAlister (1880–1953), a Canadian evangelist, baptized converts using the formula 'in the name of Jesus' (Acts 2:38) instead of the orthodox Trinitarian form, 'in the name of the Father, the Son and the Holy Spirit' (Matthew 28:19). McAlister argued that this was the practice of the early church because Jesus was the 'name' of God, whereas 'Father, Son and Holy Spirit' were merely titles for the singular name of Jesus Christ.

Many who were present at the Los Angeles camp meeting were disturbed by what had taken place. However, one of their number, the influential American evangelist Frank Ewart (1876–1947), spent a considerable time with McAlister, who convinced him that baptizing in the name of Jesus was in fact the fulfilment of the Trinitarian creed, because Jesus is the ultimate expression of the monotheistic God.

Exactly two years after the Los Angeles meeting, on 15 April 1915, Ewart gave his first sermon on Acts 2:38 in a service at which he and Glenn Cook (1867–1948) re-baptized each other. The suggestion has been made that the text for the sermon may have been supplied by McAlister, since it was not till later that Ewart started to teach that Father, Son and Holy spirit were simply modes in which the one god operated. Their action marked the beginning of a movement that led to the re-baptism of thousands of Pentecostals. The Oneness movement spread quickly through many of the Pentecostal churches, most notably the Assemblies of God (AoG), which had been formed in 1914; and in Indianapolis Cook baptized the prominent black preacher Garfield T. Haywood (1880–1931) together with over 400 members of his congregation. In response, the General Council of the AoG in 1916 debated and defeated the movement. They adopted a *Statement of Fundamental Truths* that made it a requirement that all their ministers be fully committed to Trinitarian theology. This resulted in 156 ministers, including Ewart, Howard Goss (1883–1964), one of the original organizers of the AoG in 1914, and Haywood, the only prominent black preacher in the AoG, leaving the church to form breakaway Oneness denominations. One of these was the General Assembly of Apostolic Assemblies (GAAA), formed in 1917. Garfield Haywood led the multiracial Pentecostal Assemblies of the World (PAW). The AoG had become an all-white denomination.

Core Beliefs

Common beliefs among the many Oneness Pentecostal church strands include:

● God is not a trinity and does not consist of three distinct persons; Father, Son and Holy Spirit are simply roles by which God manifests himself.

- The name of God is Jesus.
- Christians must be baptized by immersion in the name of Jesus alone; this 'Jesus only' formula is essential for salvation.
- Baptism must be administered by a duly ordained minister of a church that maintains Oneness theology.
- 'Full salvation is repentance, baptism in water by immersion in the name of the Lord Jesus Christ, and the baptism of the Holy Ghost with the initial sign of speaking in tongues as the Spirit gives utterance' (*UPC Statement of Fundamental Doctrine*).
- Any Christian who has received the Holy Spirit will speak with tongues; tongues are the initial sign of Spirit baptism.
- The bread and wine of communion are for believers only.
- Feet washing (John 13:4–5) is a divine institution to be practised by church members.

Recent Developments

The General Assembly of Apostolic Assemblies (GAAA) merged with the Pentecostal Assemblies of the World (PAW) in 1918. The denomination thus formed embraced both black and whites, but only until 1924, when the majority of whites withdrew. Since then the PAW has been a predominantly African-American church. The flamboyant evangelist Aimée Semple McPherson (1890–1944), born into a Salvation Army family and by 1910 the widow of a Pentecostal missionary, created a further strand by founding the International Church of the Foursquare Gospel and going on to evangelize from her own radio station.

A major step in the history of the white Oneness Pentecostal movement was taken in 1945 when the Pentecostal Church

Incorporated, with many former AoG members, merged with the Pentecostal Assemblies of Jesus Christ to form the United Pentecostal Church International (UPCI) with Howard Goss as the first general superintendent. Beginning with 617 churches in 1946, the UPCI currently has 25,238 churches with a membership of over 3 million. The UPCI is the largest Oneness group in North America (USA and Canada), where it has 4,142 churches. It is also found in more than 170 other nations. Oneness Pentecostals are found across the world and it is estimated that they may account for a quarter of all Pentecostal churches.

Present Practice

Oneness Pentecostals place a strong emphasis on holy living. Some consider that this leads to unnecessary legalism, which can be seen, for example, in edicts that insist that women wear skirts and abstain from using makeup. During worship services women are required to have their heads covered and men are expected to be well dressed preferably with jackets and ties. Oneness churches are of the view that television and the cinema are damaging to a person's spiritual life. Sunday worship is lively and fervent with exuberant singing, clapping and sometimes speaking in tongues and prayers for healing. There is also a strong emphasis on tithing.

24. The Order of the Solar Temple

Origins

The popularity of best-selling novels such as Umberto Eco's *Foucault's Pendulum* (1988) and Dan Brown's *The Da Vinci Code* (2003) points to a widespread casual interest in secret societies with links to the Knights Templar, but active neo-Templar groups exist in many parts of the contemporary world. Although there are significant differences between them, they all have their roots in the twelfth-century monastic and chivalric Order of the Temple and remember how its leaders were burned at the stake as heretics in the early fourteenth century. The Order of the Solar Temple (OST) was co-founded by Joseph Di Mambro (1924–94) who according to his followers in a previous life had actually been a member of the Knights Templar during the period of the Crusades. His Order derives its name from the great importance the group attaches to the sun. Members follow a version of Christianity that is mixed with New Age thinking (*see New Age Religion) and homeopathic medicine.

In his early life Di Mambro was interested in esoteric spirituality. He became a member of the Ancient and Mystical Order of the Rosae Crucis (AMORC) in 1956 and remained in membership until 1969. He continued to be influenced by AMORC's teaching and practice for the rest of his life (*see

Rosicrucianism). In 1973 he founded the Centre for the Preparation of the New Age, becoming a full-time spiritual master in 1976. His group purchased a house in France, close to Geneva, where they lived communally and practised esoteric ceremonies. In 1978 Di Mambro founded a further group in Geneva called The Golden Way. This organization combined the ideas of chivalry and a world in transformation. Di Mambro, by this time running low on emotional energy, began to look for a charismatic leader who could help to expand his movement. He met Luc Jouret (1947–94), who had previously been the charismatic leader of a group known as the Arch, and in 1984 they founded the Order of the Solar Temple. Jouret not only had charisma, he was also a medical doctor, whose views would be taken seriously. The plan was that Jouret would attract large numbers of new members into the movement by lecturing and speaking on the radio. From the beginning of their joint enterprise Jouret gave seminars and presentations in Switzerland, France and Canada.

During their ceremonies Di Mambro and Jouret's followers wore representations of the crusaders' dress and venerated a sword which Di Mambro claimed had been given to him a thousand years previously. Di Mambro's ritual began with a kind of guided meditation in which the group were invited to visualize luminous particles which flowed in and out of their bodies bringing about purification and regeneration. Next they recited *The Great Invocation*, a prayer invoking God's light and love that was received by Alice Bailey (1880–1949) in a revelation and is said by people of all faiths. This was followed by a prayer of preparation and a reading of the beginning of John's gospel.

Although the group were concerned about the environment

and pollution of the atmosphere, there was little indication in the 1980s that they had any desire to leave the planet or were even contemplating exit by suicide. Nevertheless, the possibility of such a departure was inherent in their doctrine. Members believed that they were 'noble travellers who were passing through this planet waiting to be taken back to their true home'. Di Mambro asserted that his son Elie (b. 1969) was the product of theogamy and that his daughter Emmanuelle was a 'cosmic child' who had been conceived without sex.

While Di Mambro was the power behind the throne, much of the Solar Temple's organization was undertaken by Luc Jouret. Jouret was born in the Belgian Congo, but spent his early years near Liege and studied medicine at the Free University in Brussels. After three years in general practice he became a homeopathic doctor. A former Temple member, Krishna Macharia, recalled that Jouret developed a keen interest in the spiritual healers in the Philippines and made frequent trips to Manilla to study their methods. Jouret and his wife lived in a French village close to the Swiss border, where he practised homeopathic medicine until emigrating to Canada in 1986. Following investigations by the Montreal police, it emerged that Di Mambro had also moved from his native France to Canada, as a result of tax problems, and had been convicted there for practising psychology without a licence. Other OST members had been shopping for handguns fitted with silencers.

Di Mambro firmly believed that his destiny was to lead his following through death to Sirius or a planet near it. When in 1991 the Canadian police started investigating their activities, the Order moved back to Switzerland as ecologists conducting research into macrobiotic farming. The situation did not improve for Di Mambro and his following. Some of the members began to withdraw from OST activities and ask for the large sums of money they had contributed to be returned. Di Mambro claimed he was merely a representative of the 'Masters in Zurich', but some doubted whether they existed. Adding to the pressures on him, his son Elie revealed that trickery had been used to produce spiritual phenomena during the secret ceremonial gatherings. Di Mambro and Jouret made preparations for the group to 'transit' to another world. Even Di Mambro's daughter, by the time she turned twelve in 1994, was rebelling against her father's rigid regime.

Core Beliefs

● The primacy of the spiritual over the temporal.
● Contributing to the union of the Christian churches.
● Working for the meeting of Christianity and Islam.
● The world heading for environmental catastrophe and an ending in fire.
● Luc Jouret as a manifestation of Jesus.
● Death as the ultimate stage of personal growth.
● The purification of OST members through the ritual death experience with 'Christic fire' and their return to the Grand White Lodge of Sirius (perhaps on a planet near Sirius).

Recent Developments

As the movement started to arouse the suspicions of the police and attract a spate of negative publicity in the media, they increasingly withdrew from the outside world. In its place they constructed a world of their own, which was informed by the mystical ceremonials of the Knights Templar and a growing belief that they had a vital cosmic mission to fulfil. There was a strong belief that the world would end in fire and that to transit to another planet they must die in fire. It is often the case that, when an intensive religious group begins to experience a downward spiral, they turn to an apocalyptic narrative as the only way forward. On the other hand, if Di Mambro and Jouret intended to survive, this may simply have been their way of dispensing with those who had entrusted them with large sums of money.

The movement largely came to an end in the early morning of 4 October 1994 in two house fires about three hours apart, both within fifty miles of Geneva: in a burning farmhouse at Cheiry eighteen died; in three adjacent ski chalets in Granges-sur-Salvan a further twenty-five lost their lives, including both Di Mambro and Jouret, the latter being identified by his dental records. The fires had been started deliberately and at first mass suicide was suspected. However, many of the dead were found with plastic bags over their heads and showed signs of having been involved in a struggle; some had been shot in the head as many as eight times; and a gun found in the charred chalets had been used earlier at Cheiry.

A third incident about the same time, in Canada, was clearly murder. Shortly before the fires in Switzerland Tony Dutoit, a former member, had spoken out against the group. He and his wife and baby were savagely stabbed to death at Morin Heights ski resort, Quebec Province. In their burnt-out flat, owned by Joseph Di Mambro, police discovered the bodies of two other OST members from Switzerland.

In December 1995 the death tally rose to 69. A further thirteen adults and three children were found not far from Grenoble in south-east France, fourteen of the bodies arranged in a wheel-like pattern with their heads outward, one woman's jaw fractured. On 20 March 1997, the day of the spring equinox, the bodies of another five OST members were found burned in St Casimir, a village west of Quebec City, Canada. The five had failed in a first suicide attempt owing to faulty incendiary equipment. Two teenage sons and a daughter convinced their parents that they wanted to live and were allowed to leave, while the adults succeeded in their second attempt and burned the house down.

It appears that, towards the end, relations between the two leaders became strained. On the last day of his life Di Mambro passed a letter to Patrick Vuarnet, together with his mother, an OST member, and her husband Jean, a successful businessman and Olympic ski champion, winner of the 1960 downhill gold medal in Squaw Valley. The letter stated, 'Following the tragic transit at Cheiry, we insist on specifying, in the name of the Rose+Cross, that we deplore and totally disassociate ourselves from the barbarous conduct of Dr Luc Jouret. He is the cause of veritable carnage.'

The movement's high point is generally reckoned to be January 1989 when there were 442 members: 187 in France, 90 in Switzerland, 86 in Canada, 53 in Martinique, 16 in the USA and 10 in Spain. Membership was already in decline at the time of the deaths in 1994. The Order of the Solar Temple continues to exist and is believed to have 30 surviving members in Quebec and more than 140 worldwide.

Present Practice

From the outset the social composition of the order of the Solar Temple was unusual. Intensive new religious movements are most frequently composed of young people. The bulk of the Order's members were and are solidly middle-class Swiss and Canadian citizens. Some were people of considerable ability, among them Camille Pilet, a recently retired senior executive of a multinational Swiss watch company, and Robert Ostiguy, who was for a time mayor of Richelieu in Quebec Province. There are surviving members who still believe that the miraculous apparitions and supernatural phenomena at the secret ceremonies were not faked, but genuine. Believers continue preparing for the return of Christ in Solar glory. There are no sacred texts such as the Bible or the Qur'an, but followers give serious consideration to Jouret's book, *Medicine and Conscience,* and his audio cassette, *Fundamental Time of Life: Death.*

25. Rajneesh/Osho International

Origins

The Osho Movement was founded by Bhagwan Shree Rajneesh (1931–90). He was the oldest of twelve children born in Kuchwada, Madhya Pradesh, India, to Swami Devateerth Bharti and Ma Amrit Saraswati. They named him Rajneesh Chandra Mohan and raised him in Jainism. He changed his name for the first time to Bhagwan Shree Rajneesh in 1972, which for a time resulted in his following being called Rajneeshism. During a visit to Poona in 1985 he changed his name to Osho, since when the group has been known as the Osho Movement.

Rajneesh displayed a deep interest in religion from his early childhood days and this was further enhanced during his time Jabalpur University, where he read Philosophy. He claimed to have been enlightened at the age of twenty-one. After finishing his master's degree, he taught for a number of years at Madhya State University. In 1966 he experienced 'enlightenment' and in consequence left the university to become a guru. For the next eight years he travelled across India lecturing and teaching, during which time he gained something of a reputation as 'India's sex guru'. In 1974 he opened the Bhagwan Shree Rajneesh ashram in Poona, which for the next seven years was inundated with visitors including 50,000 pilgrims from the USA.

They included hippies and drop-outs as well as spiritual seekers. They were drawn by Rajneesh's meditational practices, which featured a unique breathing exercise. Osho believed that women were spiritually superior to men and male disciples were encouraged to develop their 'inner feminine'. He believed that women also made good administrators. Women have always held the majority of leadership posts in the movement, which is unusual in any religion, East or West.

In 1981, following tax evasion charges, Rajneesh made a rapid exit to the USA, where for $6 million he purchased the extensive Big Muddy ranch fifteen miles south-west of Antelope, Oregon. Here he invested millions as, with his followers, he constructed 'a new city for a new man', known as 'Rajneeshpuram'. The focus of the new venture was very much on the prosperous sections of US society, who had both the money and the time to sample spiritual retreats and conferences. Many settled in the community, but residence came at high price; the agricultural and environmental projects needed considerable financial input, as did Rajneesh's taste for cars and aeroplanes. He had at least eleven Rolls Royces, some say as many as 93, and four aeroplanes.

One of Osho's mottoes was 'life, love, laughter'. Yet what many people anticipated would be a place of love, compassion and a genuine spiritual retreat proved to be a dysfunctional and damaging community. Some in the county demanded its closure. Rajneesh actively promoted a regime of unrestricted liberty, including free and open sex, which resulted in widespread incidences of sexually transmitted diseases. There were accusations of abuse, as members were virtually forced to engage in building and construction work for long hours with little or no pay. The management structures became increasingly dictatorial; almost everywhere in Rajneeshpuram was reported to be electronically bugged, on Osho's instructions, even the tables in the communal dining halls; and members were encouraged to report fellow members who did not comply with Osho's instructions.

By the mid-1980s the 'new city' had taken on the appearance of a military encampment, with armed security guards and inquisitional tactics. An Indian woman originally employed as Rajneesh's secretary, Ma Anand Sheela, had progressively taken control of the entire movement. Serious accusations were made against her regarding phone-tapping and involvement in an attempt to murder Rajneesh's doctor. She fled to Germany in 1985, was extradited, and served twenty-nine months in a federal prison. Rajneesh denounced her as a dictator, but it was too late to save the situation. He was forced to close Rajneeshpuram in September 1985 and tried to flee the country the following month. When his plane halted for refuelling, he was stopped, arrested, fined $400,000 and subsequently expelled from the country.

Core Beliefs

● God is not a person but a presence that resides in everything, including human beings.
● Spiritual development is achieved by freeing oneself from all socialization and taking up a programme of meditation and therapy drawn largely from the Human Potential Movement.
● Enlightenment (Christhood) can be reached through sex and meditation.
● Jesus became Christ on the cross.

- When Jesus spoke of fulfilling the scriptures (Matthew 26:54, Mark 14:49), Osho asserted that he was referring to the Hindu scriptures.
- Jesus died at the age of 112 in Kashmir.

Recent Developments

Osho succeeded in combining Eastern meditation with Western psychosexual and holistic therapies. In doing so he came to have a significant impact on Western spirituality in the later 1970s and 1980s. In his later years Osho lived in poor health and suffered from myalgic encephalomyelitis (ME). He also had type 2 diabetes, asthma and severe back pain, which resulted in his becoming addicted to prescription drugs. He was constantly sick and several people who knew him well believe that he died of AIDS as a result of having unprotected sex with many different partners.

Membership numbers have fluctuated a good deal. The Osho web site reported 250,000 adherents in 1982. The number of committed devotees was more likely of the order of 30,000. At the height of Osho's Movement there were about 600 centres worldwide, but these had dwindled to about 20 by the time of his death. However, he still has influence through his books and other materials available on the web. Current adherents are estimated to be fewer than 10,000.

Present Practice

Osho followed the Buddhist tantric masters in his advocacy of sexual intercourse as a means of encountering the divine. His followers were initiated as disciples in a ceremony which was essentially the ritual for *sanyassins* (devoted Hindu men). It originally involved taking a new name, being clad in an orange robe, wearing a *mala* with a locket containing Osho's picture and keeping at least one period of meditation each day. In the later years of the movement only the last of these four was retained.

The most important ceremony for Osho's following was the evening worship session (*darshana*). This was radically changed from the traditional Hindu meditative style to 'an energy *darshan*', which employed loud music and flashing lights and made use of female 'mediums' to heighten the energy levels of the worshippers. Since Osho's death in 1990 this ceremony, now known as The Brotherhood of the White Rose, has become a daily ritual.

26.   Rastafarianism

Origins

The word 'ras' means 'prince' and 'Tafari' is the name of an Ethiopian royal house in the same way that 'Windsor' is the designation of the family of Queen Elizabeth II. Rastafarianism, often referred to as Rasta, first emerged in the 1930s in the deprived quarters of Kingston, Jamaica, since when African-Caribbean people have carried it to North America, western Europe and Australia and New Zealand. It has made a significant impact in Jamaica and the UK.

The beginnings of the movement go back to the years immediately following the liberation of the slaves in Britain's colonies in 1834, during which there was a rapid growth of specifically black churches. Not surprisingly, the freed slaves began to look to their African homeland as the place where their ancestors were free. In particular, their focus settled on the country of Ethiopia as a great centre of culture and the one nation that had never been colonized by the white man. One of those who drew on this heritage was the Jamaican-born Marcus Garvey (1887–1940), who with four friends founded The Negro Improvement Association in 1914 with the aim of giving the world's black peoples independence from white society. In order to foster this objective Garvey travelled extensively in the USA, settling in New

York City in 1917, where he established the African Orthodox Church along with The Black Star Line shipping company that he anticipated would eventually take his followers back to Africa.

In his preaching Garvey urged his hearers to 'Look to Africa for the crowning of a black king; he shall be the redeemer.' This message seemed to many to be powerfully endorsed in 1930, when Haile Selassie (1892–1975) was crowned emperor of Ethiopia, and again when he returned to the throne in 1941 on the defeat of the invading Italians. His family claimed a line that stretched back to Menelik I, son of Solomon and Queen Makeda of Sheba, and his full title was: Ras Tafari, son of Ras Makonnen of Harar, King of Ethiopia, Haile Selassie ('power of the Trinity'), King of Kings, Lord of Lords, Conquering Lion of the Tribe of Judah. For the downtrodden people who followed Garvey, descendents of slaves and still subject to segregation or racial discrimination in the USA, the crowning of this young Ethiopian king with a biblical title was a revelation from God himself. With the passing of time they came to regard him as a revelation of 'the living God'.

Garvey's teachings were taken up by a number of others including Archibald Dunkley, who proclaimed Haile Selassie as *the* messiah, and Leonard Howell (1898–1960), who established the Rastafarian Pinnacle community north-west of Kingston, where a number of key rituals were introduced, including the smoking of *ganja* (marijuana) at meetings, men adopting dreadlocks and women plaiting their hair.

Core Beliefs

Rastafarianism is an extremely diverse movement. There were three main groups in the British Isles by the 1970s: the Universal

Black Improvement Organisation, the Twelve Tribes of Israel, the Ethiopian World Federation. More recently two other groups, the Prince Emmanuel and the Boboshantis, have established themselves in parts of England. The Twelve Tribes, founded in 1968 by Vernon Carrington, has some distinctly Christian aspects that the others do not share. The following core ideals are shared by most Rastafarians:

● Haile Selassie, Emperor of Ethiopia, is 'the true and living God' and is referred to as 'Jah'. The Twelve Tribes differ on this point, believing that Jesus is essential to salvation and that only after a person has received his forgiveness can they see in Haile Selassie a reflection of Christ.

● God is black and the true Israelites are black.

● Blacks will ultimately rule the world.

● They will be established in Ethiopia before the cataclysmic end-time conflict at Armageddon.

● The Bible is the main authority, but much of it is interpreted allegorically.

Recent Developments

By the close of 1954 there were at least twelve Rastafarian groups in Kingston alone, ranging in size from 20 to 150, and there were nightly rituals of singing and dancing. In 1958 the different groups held their first Rastafarian Universal Convention. Rastafarian morale received a huge boost when his Imperial Majesty, Haile Selassie, made a scheduled stop in Jamaica. Although his visit was unconnected in any way with the Rastafarians, an estimated 10,000 Rastas were in the crowd who greeted him at the airport calling out 'Hosanna to the

Son of David'. Since that time Rastafarianism has grown considerably. Their numbers were estimated between 70,000 and 100,000 in 1970, the majority less than 35 years of age. Their current membership is estimated to be around 200,000 with 14,000 in the USA and 5,000 in Britain. Additionally, there are considerable numbers of sympathizers, especially in Jamaica.

In the post war years significant numbers of African-Caribbeans settled in the UK and other European countries. The United Afro-West Indian Brotherhood was first observed in London in 1955. The movement was further strengthened by the commitment of Robert (Bob) Marley (1945–1981), whose reggae music so well expressed their aspirations. Many blacks adopted Rasta dress, customs and ideals without necessarily being committed to the core beliefs about salvation through a black messiah.

Present Practice

Most Rastafarians see worship primarily as an individual and personal affair, rather than a corporate experience. Members of the Twelve Tribes are required to read a chapter of the Bible a day. They are encouraged to pray individually and hold meetings for different purposes with their family/Rastafarian groups. These may be weekly, monthly or quarterly. In recent times the Twelve Tribes have been meeting every three months. On these occasions twenty-four chapters of the Bible will be read, with twelve men and twelve women from each of the Twelve Tribes reading a chapter each. Each reader will also give a brief testimony. Usually three hymns are sung and there are prayers for the sick and needy. Baptism for the Twelve

Tribes is seen as a 'baptism of fire', the fire being a symbol of purification.

A controversial aspect of Rastafarian denominations is the smoking of ganja, which is spoken of as the 'wisdom weed'. This has both a religious and social function. The smoke which rises from the chillum pipes is believed to be sending up incense to Jah. The practice draws on such texts as Genesis 1:12, which speaks of the earth bringing forth grass 'and God saw that it was good'. Rastafarians have an emphasis on festivals, although they do not keep Christmas or Easter. The Twelve Tribes celebrate four major days in the year: the founding of the Organisation of African Unity on 25 May, Haile Selassie's birthday on 23 July, Haile Selassie's state visit to England on 14 October, and his coronation on 2 November.

Rastafarians grow their hair long for a variety of reasons. For some it is a symbol of submission to Jah. The word 'dread' means rebellion, so for many Rastas their long locks are a sign of their rejection of white culture. As true Israelites, strict Rastafarians observe the Old Testament dietary laws and do not drink alcohol, milk or tea.

27.   Rosicrucianism/AMORC

Origins

Rosicrucianism is a diverse occult grouping of organizations with members in Britain and across Europe and the USA. Some are highly secretive and others are linked with the Freemasons or require membership of the Freemasons. Others such as AMORC (the Ancient and Mystical Order of the Rosae Crucis) make information freely available on the internet. Their common symbol is a Christian cross with a red rose in the centre, chosen because of their ancient occult significance. The cross is held to be a symbol of the sun, the generator force and the male element; the rose represents the feminine and depicts beauty and delicacy.

The precise origins of Rosicrucianism are obscure and its organizations draw on a number of ancient Egyptian and Gnostic traditions as well as astrology, alchemy, mysticism and parapsychology.

The term 'Rosicrucianism' first appeared in English in *The Praiseworthy Order of the Rosae Crucis*, the translation of *Fama Fraternitatis*, published in Kassel, Germany, in 1614 by the Lutheran theologian Johann Valentine Andreae (1586–1654), grandson of Jakob Andreae (1528–90), himself a theologian and Chancellor of Tübingen University. There had been lots of brotherhoods of monks and nuns (*fraternitates, confraternitates, sodalitates*) in Germany a century or so earlier, such as the Dominican Rosenkranzbruderschaft of Cologne, founded in 1475. However, the Order of the Rosae Crucis was different.

Shortly after the publication of *Fama Fraternitatis* Andreae produced two further texts on the subject, *Confessio Fraternitatis* (*The Confession of the Rosicrucian Fraternity*) and *Chymische Hochzeit Christiani Rosencreutz* (*The Chemical Marriage of Christian Rosenkreuz*). According to his trilogy, the Rosicrucian brotherhood was founded in 1408 by Christian Rosenkreuz (1378–1484), a former monk and German nobleman, who had been initiated into Arabian magical practices while travelling through Damascus, Jerusalem and Fez. At an unknown location in the Holy Land, but possibly under the Temple Mount itself, Rosenkreuz was initiated into a secret, esoteric order which was a precursor to the Rosae Crucis. The symbol of the rosy cross was chosen because the rose and cross were ancient occult symbols and were on his family arms. Apparently Andreae's ideal religion was an anti-papal form of Christianity tinged with theosophy. He openly mocked alchemistic occultism and frequently described as 'a ridiculous comedy' the host of pseudo-occult societies that Rosicrucianism spawned.

The appearance of Andreae's pamphlets prompted the production of literature from the pen of Robert Fludd (1574–1637), an Oxford physician, who in 1616 published a defence of the Brotherhood of the Rosy Cross entitled *Apologia Compendiaria Fraternitatem de Rosea Cruce*. In consequence several new Rosicrucian societies emerged in Europe. The aim was that their names should appear in *The Book of Life*, which records all the successive incarnations of each human being and to this end they gave themselves to the study of the hidden forces of nature.

A significant aspect of this devotion was their annual assembly at their secret headquarters, the Edifice of the Holy Spirit.

Core Beliefs

- God is impersonal and understood as supreme intelligence and a form of pure energy.
- Jesus is not fully God, but is the highest initiate of the moon period and a source of all knowledge lying beyond the material universe.
- The number 7 is highly significant. At birth the child possesses a dense body, at 7 years of age a vital body, at 14 a desire body and at 21 the mind is formed.
- Within every individual there resides a deeper nature or personality that has unbelievable potential. As an initiate learns to tap into this inner self, he or she learns to be guided by 'the still, small voice within'.
- The supreme goal of the Rosicrucian Order is a permanent awareness of the unity all creation, a personal relationship with the oneness of the universe and 'a direct experience of the profound attunement with the Divinity which religions and philosophies of all ages have so forcefully alluded'.

Recent Developments

In the nineteenth century there was a renewed interest in Rosicrucianism and a cluster of new societies came into being. Among them were the Fraternitas Rosae Crucis (1858), the Societas Rosicruciana in Anglia (1865), which requires its members to be Freemasons, and the Rosicrucian Fellowship founded by Max Heindel (1865–1919) in 1907. The most prominent of the present day Rosicrucian groups is the Ancient and Mystical Order of the Rosae Crucis (AMORC), which was founded in 1915 by Harvey Spencer Lewis (1883–1939), an author and occult practitioner, born in New York City, where he had founded the New York Institute for Psychical Research in 1904. In 1917 a major conference was held which drew up plans to convey the movement's teachings by means of correspondence course.

There are Roscicrucian chapters throughout the world, including the USA, where there are more than a hundred affiliated groups. In the UK there are some 25 groups, with headquarters at Crowborough, East Sussex. Recent statistics for Australia indicated that there were 14 centres with 1,582 members. Rosicrucians have 1,500 centres worldwide with an estimated 250,000 members.

Present Practice

The Rosicrucian order is open to people of every race, creed and culture. Members are encouraged to set up an altar at home with candles, incense and Egyptian deities, most importantly the sun god Ra. Members are exhorted to contact departed spirit masters in 'psychic contacts with soul personalities' who are now part of the 'Universal Soul'. Adherents in effect become mediums.

Some Rosicrucians, both men and women, attend temples that resemble masonic lodges (*see* Freemasonry). The Master of the lodge sits at one end of the room and the Matre of the lodge, a woman, sits at the other end. The vestal virgin ignites the incense from a sacred flame. Members wear aprons similar to those used by Freemasons and before their initiation they swear an oath of secrecy. The teaching is divided into degrees that are grouped into broad categories under titles such as The Neophite, The Postulant and The Temple. Each degree consists of lessons that are issued on a weekly basis so they can be studied in the home. Two special feasts are kept, the New Year Feast in March and the Outdoor Fête in September.

Rosicrucians utilize a whole range of techniques that are all designed to bring the initiate to experience enlightenment. These include effective concentration, contemplation, meditation and visualization. Members are also taught how to speed up the natural healing processes in their bodies. AMORC publishes two magazines: *Rosicrucian Digest* and *The Rosicrucian Forum*, a members-only publication.

28.   Sahaja Yoga

Origins

Sahaja Yoga was first taught in 1970 by Shri Mataji Nirmala Devi and has spread around the world. Usually known simply as Mataji, its founder was born of wealthy Protestant Christian parents in Chindwara, India, on 21 March 1923 and married Sri Chandrika Prasad Srivastava, joint-secretary to the Indian prime ministers in the 1960s and later a high-ranking official in the United Nations.

Mataji was originally a disciple of Osho (*see* Rajneesh/Osho International), but she fell out with him and set up her own movement. *Sahaja* ('spontaneity') is a distinctive type of yoga that its adherents believe gives them a greater sense of 'self-realization'. The goal of Sahaja Yoga is to achieve 'thoughtless awareness', in which the mind is cleared of all background noises and distraction and becomes clear 'like a mountain stream'. Mataji claimed to have experienced 'full realization' on 5 May 1970 and began to work as a healer. This self-realization is achieved when the individual connects with the eternal spirit that is held to reside within every member of the human race. Members are taught that it is not the body, mind or ego which are of primary importance, but rather the eternal spirit within. Practitioners of Sahaja Yoga say that they can actually feel the release of this divine presence and power coming on them like a cool breeze.

In earlier times only a very few individuals seemed to be able to achieve inner cleansing and greater self-realization and that after many years of practising yoga. Mataji's method enables the individual to achieve self-realization spontaneously (*sahaja*). The experience is also termed 'second birth' or 'enlightenment'. In Mataji's system the individual becomes his or her own guru and is able, through self-realization, to release spiritual energy (*kundalini*) which lies dormant at the base of the spine in the sacrum bone. *Kundalini* is released through six energy points (*chakras*) above the sacrum as it travels up the spine and is released through the fontanelle at the top of the head as 'a gentle fountain of coolness'. This enables the practitioner to clear away any subsequent further blockages to higher spiritual awareness that may occur. Such blockages can be felt in the fingertips.

Practitioners of Sahaja Yoga claim to be able to clear the unwanted thoughts that constantly seek to invade their minds. This enables them to live lives that are more focused and relaxed. The new state of being, which is referred to as 'thoughtless awareness', generates deep peace and joy.

Core Beliefs

Sahaja Yoga draws on the basic teachings of Hinduism, including the doctrines of karma and reincarnation. The core beliefs are set out in three seminal texts, Shri Mataji's *Meta Modern Era* and *The Advent* (1979) and Grégoire de Kalbermatten's *The Third Advent* (2003).

- The character of a variety of deities can be felt in the individual's energy points (*chakras*).
- Laksmi, the wife of the god Vishnu, is the ideal on which female disciples are to model themselves.
- Shri Mataji is the perfect embodiment of the feminine root power that materializes the universe.
- Commitment to Shri Mataji can enable any person to awaken their spiritual energy and this can lead on to his or her enlightenment.
- Shri Mataji is the avatar of the supreme goddess or primordial power (Adi Shakti).

Recent Developments

Like many other new religious institutions, Sahaja Yoga has engaged in a variety of humanitarian and charitable ventures, including work among the very poor and dying, cancer research and a hospital where Sahaja Yoga methods of healing are used. Mataji has come to be regarded with increasing respect and devotion. Whilst in London on 2 December 1979 she declared herself to be divine. Many of her followers regard her as Devi, the Indian goddess who comes to save the world. Photographs of her are used as symbols in meditation and on occasion practitioners express their indebtedness in the Hindu ritual of pouring a 'nectar' of honey or cow's milk over her feet, which is kept and drunk.

There are estimated to be 20,000 members in 60 countries across the world. Outside of India there are Sahaja Yoga centres in most western European nations as well as in Canada and the USA. There are 36 centres in Australia with an estimated 550 members.

Present Practice

Unlike many new religious groups, Sahaja Yoga is led by a woman, but it is neither feminist nor matriarchal. Women members, in keeping with Hindu traditions, are exhorted to be both feminine and submissive. Mataji proclaims herself as a role model for wives. The movement's leadership is almost entirely in the hands of men.

Sahaja Yoga is easily accessible and Mataji makes no charges for her lectures, insisting that you cannot pay for your enlightenment. Many free courses are offered at local centres in countries across the world. An individual can even sit down in front of a computer and try out the various techniques on his or her own. The more affluent middle-class adherents are able to make regular donations to pay for her overseas lecture tours and to finance the purchase of major properties in England, Italy and elsewhere. Committed followers refer to Shri Mataji as the Divine Mother (*mata ji*) and she herself has adopted the title 'Primal Mother of All'. Many seek her advice and guidance on a wide range of issues, including in some instances the choice of a marriage partner. Shri Mataji has conducted mass weddings in India.

There is great stress on cleanliness, requiring frequent hand-washing, brushing the teeth twice a day and gargling with salt water to prevent throat illnesses. Devotees also rub their scalps with oil once a week to keep it sufficiently soft for the *kundalini* to pass through. Members engage in a variety of rituals, among which is shoe beating. This entails drawing a circle on the ground with the right index finger and then symbolically circling into it something that is of concern. That done, the left shoe is taken in the right hand and the ground gently beaten with the heel either 21 or 108 times. This practice is believed to remove obstacles to a person's spiritual development.

29.   The Satya Sai Baba Society

Origins

The Satya Sai Baba Society was founded by Sai Baba. He was born on 23 November 1926 in Puttaparthi, Andhra Pradesh, the fourth child of a father who was a distinguished actor, and named Sathyanarayanan Raju, which means 'true, all-pervading God'. In 1940 a scorpion bit him and his subsequent trance-like behaviour caused his parents such concern that they consulted an exorcist. Shortly after this incident he began to materialize sweets and flowers, subsequently announcing himself as the incarnation of an earlier guru, Shirdi Sai Baba (1838–1918), and inviting the assembled group to worship him every Thursday. Soon he discarded his schoolbooks and left his family. He began to perform what appeared to many to be startling miracles and his reputation grew rapidly, such that on 23 November 1950 he established an ashram outside his home village of Puttaparthi.

In 1961 he inaugurated the era of Sai truth (Satya Sai Era) and four years later established an academy for Vedic and Sanskrit studies. In 1967 he organized the first All-India Conference of Sathya Sai Baba and followed this with a world conference in 1968. In the same year he was instrumental in founding a college for women at Anantapur in the state of Andhra Pradesh. These developments reached their climax on the 1 October 1976 when he proclaimed the foundation of the Sai religion, which he declared to be 'the essence of all religions'.

Core Beliefs

Sai Baba teaching is essentially Hinduism in a simplified form but with the guru accorded divine status.

● Ordinary individuals are born according to their karma.
● Certain holy figures, such as Sai Baba, are freed from their karma.
● To gain liberation from the circle of life, death and rebirth necessitates a combination of wisdom, good deeds and regular devotion.
● All are equal regardless of caste, creed, race or gender.
● One should seek not to harm any living being (and thus vegetarianism is preferable).
● Holy love (*prema*) should be expressed to fellow human beings and, especially, to Sai Baba.
● Baba is a full avatar of God, the embodiment of Shiva and Shakti.

Recent Developments

By the mid-1970s Satya Sai centres began to be established in the USA as the result of individuals who travelled to Puttaparthi and subsequently became devotees.

The Sai Baba Society has four main concerns: the cultivation of the *Vedas* (Aryan scriptures) and science and the practice of devotion (*bhakti*) and service (*dharma*). The cultivation of the

Vedas means the carrying out of Vedic rituals, including the singing of religious songs (*bhajana*) and saying mantras.

Sai Baba's distinctive, non-Brahminical appearance and his society that actively seeks to transcend the caste system have been particularly appealing to those on the Indian sub-continent. By 1979 there were, according to official Satya sources, 3,800 communities across India and nearly 20,000 trained members with over 35,000 in the Sai Society's school programme. At that time the total number of followers was stated to be more than 2 million.

From the 1980s onwards Bhagavan Sri Sai Baba came to occupy an increasingly dominant role over his many followers. He is widely held to be an avatar of God and the saviour of the human race. Sai Baba himself is reported to have said, 'I am the omnipresent, almighty and omniscient.' He interprets his name (Sai) as both 'divine Mother' and 'divine Father'. Vast numbers have travelled to his most important ashram at Puttaparthi. Today he has millions of devotees on the Indian sub-continent as well as in Europe and North America.

Sai Baba has a huge reputation as a miracle worker and materializes watches, flowers, crucifixes, books, photographs and above all holy ashes (*vibhuti*) with the wave of the hand. There are constant reports too of astounding healings performed with the help of the ashes. However, a growing number of critics are of the view that many of his materializations amount to mere con tricks.

Present Practice

The Sai Baba Society has a major concern for education and particularly that of women. It also actively encourages lay members to engage in voluntary service and work to break down the caste system. Devotees are exhorted to practise meditation on a daily basis. The recommended time for a working person is half an hour of sitting meditation both mornings and evenings. To aid concentration, individuals are advised to use a mantra (a sound which is chanted) and an object on which to focus, such as a lighted candle or a sacred picture of Rama, Krishna or Jesus.

In the case of those who are close to Sai Baba and give all their time to the movement, there are more strenuous religious exercises. These may include tantric kundalini yoga, which utilizes physical sensations, including sex, in order to awaken deeper levels of spiritual power and awareness.

30.   Sôka Gakkai International

Origins

Sôka Gakkai, which means 'value-creating society', is a lay organization of individuals who practise a form of Buddhism first taught by the monk Nichiren (1222–82), who was born in the village of Kashiwazaki in Niigata Prefecture in Japan. The group was founded in 1930 by Tsunesaburo Makiguchi (1871–1944). It has its headquarters in Tokyo with an American base at Santa Barbara, California, and an English centre at Taplow, near London. Nichiren was concerned that a number of different strands of Buddhist teaching had emerged and therefore set himself the task of distilling the heart or central core of the Buddha's teaching. He reached the conclusion that it could be summed up in the *Lotus Sutra*, which the Buddha had composed sometime in the years immediately preceding his death (in the fifth century BCE). Nichiren taught the people that they could attain enlightenment by chanting the *Lotus Sutra*. Sôka Gakkai International (SGI) does not offer a specific behaviour code or demand a particular lifestyle; rather it seeks to build people's faith by chanting the title phrase of the sutra, *nam-myoho-renge-kyo*, morning and evening and by studying the writings of Nichiren. Members also deepen their commitment by sharing their experiences with one another.

Core Beliefs

● All living beings have the potential to attain enlightenment or Buddhahood; with faith Sôka Gakkai members can achieve this.

● Past actions influence the present; present actions influence the future (*karma*).

● Each thought, word and deed has an immediate effect both on the individual and on his or her environment.

● All the benefits contained in the *Lotus Sutra* can be obtained by chanting its title phrase: *nam-myoho-renge-kyo* ('Hail to the law of the lotus teaching').

● The daily use of the scroll (*gohonzon*), which is written in Chinese and contains the life of Nichiren and the characters of the *nam-myoho-renge-kyo* and Nichiren's signature, acts as a spiritual mirror and conveys a protective influence.

● Constant focus on three important principles: beauty (*bi*), gain (*ri*) and goodness (*zen*).

Recent Developments

During the Second World War the Japanese government banned Sôka Gakkai, fearing that it would undermine the country's war effort. Makiguchi was among those who were arrested and he died in prison. After the war was over, Josei Toda (1900–58), an educator and publisher and one of Makiguchi's closest followers, took on the leadership in 1946 and gave fresh impetus to the movement. It was during this time that the name Sôka Gakkai was adopted. The present leader is Daisaku Ikeda (b. 1928), the fifth son of a poor working-class Tokyo family, who joined the movement in 1947, having been deeply impressed by Toda's character and his firm anti-militarist stand. Toda is remembered for his uncompromising stand against nuclear weapons. When Toda died, Ikeda succeeded him as the movement's third president.

At the time of Toda's death Sôka Gakkai numbered nearly a million followers. Under the leadership of the movement's third president, Daisaku Ikeda, Sôka Gakkai's influence increased rapidly. He committed himself to continue Toda's policy 'to destroy other religions'. Ikeda emerged as a powerful figure. English journalist Polly Toynbee wrote, 'I have never in my life met a man who exuded such an aura of absolute power as Mr Ikeda.' In 1965 Sôka Gakkai organized its own political party, Komeito (the party of clean government), which at one point was Japan's third-largest party. In 1970, amid concerns about the movement's aggressive style of proselyzation (*shakubuku*) and its blurring of the separation between religion and state, Ikeda ended the formal link and tempered its methods of gaining converts.

In 1979 Ikeda resigned from the presidency of Sôka Gakkai to establish Sôka Gakkai International (SGI) and develop the movement abroad. Membership continued to expand from about 5,000 in the 1950s to over 12 million worldwide at the present time. SGI has organizations and members in 190 countries.

Present Practice

The daily practice of Nichiren's teachings is believed to have a profound effect on the quality of the everyday lives of its adherents. Regular chanting generates a confidence that helps to overcome negative impulses and thus to create an increasingly positive attitude to daily living as well as to the world in general. Members must practise their faith on a daily basis and they are encouraged to meet locally in small groups at least once a week. All SGI disciples are expected to study the letters and treatises of Nichiren, which are published in English translation as *The Major Writings of Nichiren Daishonin*. Members set aside time each morning and evening for their private devotions. This includes reciting the two most important chapters (the second and the sixteenth) of the *Lotus Sutra* and chanting the *nam-myoho-renge-kyo*. In a piece entitled *The One Essential Phrase* Nichiren wrote: 'Truly, if you chant this in the morning and the evening, you are correctly reading the entire *Lotus Sutra*.' Chanting is regarded as the way to influence and improve situations. There is no situation that cannot be chanted for. SGI members chant in front of their *gohonzon*, which is set up as a small domestic shrine. SGI publishes *The Art of Living*, a monthly magazine which offers articles of a practical nature to help members in the practice of their faith.

Sôka Gakkai has four objectives: to work for the prosperity of society as good citizens; to promote humanistic education in line with Nichiren Buddhist teaching; to support UN efforts for world peace; and to work towards solving problems of poverty, oppression and environmental destruction. Sôka Gakkai is actively involved in the world of politics and aims in this way to make the world a more peaceful and stable planet on which to live. Members therefore give frequent support to campaigns for human rights, environmental improvement and the relief of hunger and disease.

31.   Spiritualism

Origins

Spiritualism includes a variety of differing networks and groups, some of which hold some specifically Christian beliefs and others that are almost totally devoid of any religious dogma at all. They all, however, share one central concept of communication with the dead or spirit realm through gifted or psychic individuals. Spiritualists always speak of the 'departed' rather than of the 'dead'.

Early Spiritualism was very largely what today would be understood as 'physical mediumship', in which the 'spirit' operates on a physical level, perhaps lifting or turning tables, levitating objects or creating audible rappings. It also includes manifestations of ectoplasm, which is thought to be a viscous substance that sometimes appears to exude from the body during a sitting. Physical mediumship is associated with 'trance mediumship', where the medium passes into an unconscious state and is then 'possessed' by a spirit who communicates with the 'sitters' or people attending the séance.

The later nineteenth century witnessed the emergence of mediumship in which the medium remains in a state of full awareness and either sees in a parapsychological way (clairvoyant) or hears (clairaudient) and then passes on the information to the sitters. The mediumship which is practised in most spiritualist churches is almost exclusively clairvoyant.

The origins of Spiritualism stretch back into the ancient world of the Middle East. In more recent time Emmanuel Swedenborg (1688–1772) who had a remarkable gift of clairvoyance, sowed the seeds of Spiritualist thought. In the following century, two sisters, Katie and Margaret Fox, were the first people on record to have reputedly held a conversation with a spirit. This took place on 31 March 1848 at Hydesville in New York State. The resulting publicity stirred hundreds, perhaps thousands, of ordinary people to investigate the possibility of communicating with the dead. In the USA, Spiritualism is fostered by the National Spiritualist Association of Churches (NSAC), an undogmatic organization founded in 1893, with its present headquarters at Lily Dale, New York State.

Spiritualism took root in England through individuals such as the Socialist entrepreneur, Robert Owen (1771–1858), and the first Spiritualist Church in England was established by David Richmond at Keighley, Yorkshire, in 1853.

Core Beliefs

All Spiritualists believe in the following:
● The fatherhood of God, the brotherhood of man, the immortality of the soul, personal responsibility, compensation and retribution hereafter for all the good and evil deeds done here, and a path of eternal progress open to every human soul that wills to tread it by the path of eternal good.

● At death the spirit is set free from the body and is free to roam. It can then choose to go on to a higher spiritual level, reincarnate or become a spirit guide to the living.
● Guidance is received from personal spirit guides or through mediums.

Additionally, Christian Spiritualists such as The Greater World Christian Spiritualist Association believe:
● God is love and is the creator of all things.
● Jesus Christ is the exemplar for living, but did not atone for sin by his sacrificial death.
● God manifests his power through the Holy Spirit.

Recent Developments

In the twentieth century two main umbrella organizations emerged in the UK, the Spiritualist National Union that was founded in 1901 and the Greater World Christian Spiritualist League (GWCSL) that was formed in 1931. The Spiritualist National Union, with its registered office at Stansted Hall in Essex, is the larger organization, with some 382 affiliated churches and a total membership in 1996 of 20,267. The GWCSL, which subsequently changed its name to the Greater World Christian Spiritualist Association (GWCSA), emerged from the SNU partly through the influence of Sir Arthur Conan Doyle (1859–1930) and Winifred Moyes who received many messages from Zodiac, her spirit guide. The GWCSA currently has just over a hundred affiliated churches, the majority of which are situated in the south and east of the UK. However, it should be emphasized that by no means all Christian Spiritualist churches are linked to an umbrella organization. The 1996 census recorded 8,140 Spiritualists in Australia.

Present Practice

Most Christian Spiritualist churches hold several services a week. Divine worship on a Sunday normally includes clairvoyance and sometimes a short service of healing follows. Some Christian Spiritualist churches also hold services of Holy Communion that have much the same appearance as those in the denominational churches. 'The Greater World Belief and Pledge' invites members to 'accept the leadership of Jesus Christ' and makes reference to his 'redemptive power', but is nevertheless a long way removed from apostolic, creedal Christianity.

All Spiritualists, whether they adhere to a semblance of Christian belief or not, are united in the conviction that after death the spirit is set free from the individual's body. It is then free to roam and can choose to go on to a higher spiritual level or to reincarnate or to become a spirit guide to the living. The major business of Spiritualism is about helping to put congregational members in touch with spirit guides who will be of assistance to them as they run their earthly course.

32.   The Sufi Movement

Origins

'Amongst the Prophet's early followers,' to quote David Kerr, Professor of Islamic Studies, Hartford, Connecticut, 'were the so-called "people of the bench" (*'ahl al-suffa*) who rarely left the mosque in Medina [and] wore a simple tunic made of wool (suf), symbolizing their obedience to the many prophets who practised asceticism. The English word *Sufism* comes from the Arabic *tasawwuf* which could be translated as self-purification. *Sufi* (fem. *sufiyya*) denotes a person whose heart is purified from the pollution of this world. Strictly speaking a Sufi should never describe himself, nor a Sufiyya herself, by this term. They use the related word *mutasawwif* (fem. *mutasawwifa*), "one who tries to be a Sufi".'

As the word 'Sufi' has come to denote the concepts of wisdom and purity, so the primary aims of Sufism are the awakening of these two 'heart qualities' and the release of the soul from self-centred boundaries, so that it can merge into the all-pervading divine presence. However, although Sufism emerged as a mystical form of Islam, stressing a more devotional and loving relationship with God, in the present context it should be said that not all Muslim Sufis consider themselves to be mystics and many Western Sufis do not regard themselves as Muslims.

The person responsible for bringing Sufism to the West outside the confines of Islam was Inayat Khan (1882–1927), known as Hazrat (saint) Inayat Khan, who was born at Baroda, Gujarat, India, into a loving Muslim family with a strong musical tradition. His maternal grandfather, Chole Ghise Khan Maulabakhsh (1833–96), who was known as the 'Beethoven of India', had founded a musical academy that is now the Baroda University Faculty of Music. Inayat's vocal and musical skills were soon widely recognized and even before he was twenty he was playing the vina in many of the royal courts.

While still only in his twenties Inayat laid aside his musical ambitions in order to devote himself to Sufism, following the spiritual guidance of Shaikh Sayyid Muhammad Abu Hashim Madani of the Chishti Sufi order. On 13 September 1910 he left his homeland and sailed first to the USA, where he met and married Ora Ray Baker in 1912. Their first child was born in Moscow and the remaining three in England, where they sought refuge during the First World War. In the early 1920s Inayat and his family took up residence in Paris. There he gave lectures and organized summer schools for the increasing number of people who were seeking inner peace in the aftermath of military destruction. Some of the lectures which Inayat gave during these years have since been published and now form the key texts of the movement, including *The Unity of Religious Ideals, Love Human and Divine* and *Health, Mental Purification and the Mind World*. Inayat founded the International Sufi Movement in 1923 and gave himself unstintingly to spreading the Sufi message, continuing to live with his family in Paris but establishing the Sufi headquarters in Geneva. In 1926 Inayat made what he intended to be a short visit to his native India. He was unexpectedly taken ill and died in Tilak Lodge, New Delhi, on 5 February 1927. His tomb has since become a place of pilgrimage for Sufis from all over the world.

Core Beliefs

- Although rooted in the Islamic tradition, Sufism asserts that there is a common thread running through all religions and that there is only one God. There is one God, the eternal, and the only being.
- The scriptures given to the Jews, the Muslims, Parsis, Hindus, Buddhists, all have as their central truth the message of unity. Hazrat Inayat Khan wrote, 'True life cannot be ours until unity is achieved' and 'The only studies which are worth accomplishing are those which lead to the realization of God, and of unity first with God and then with the self and so with all.'
- There is one holy book, the sacred manuscript of nature, the only scripture which can enlighten the reader.
- There is one brotherhood, the human brotherhood, which unites the children of earth indiscriminately in the fatherhood of God.
- There is one moral principle, the love that springs forth from self-denial and blooms in deeds of beneficence.

Recent Developments

It was Hazrat Inayat Khan's hope and desire that his son Vilayat Khan (1916–2004) would take on the leadership of the Sufi Movement. Initially Vilayat showed no desire to do so. This led to

Inayat's brother taking the reins in 1927 and afterwards one of his cousins. In the 1960s Vilayat was ready to accede to his father's wish. However, the movement was split by his decision, so he established the Sufi Order of the West to promote his father's inner teachings.

Vilayat's Sufi Order of the West has grown considerably in recent years and attracted a growing number of adherents in Canada and the USA. Several orders of Sufism subsequently emerged from Hazrat Inayat Khan's mission and many more follow the teachings contained in his lectures. Idries Shah (1924–96) was a significant influence in fostering knowledge of Sufism in the UK and the West through his more than thirty-five books and over a hundred academic monographs. Western Sufism is strongest in Germany, where some estimates put the number of adherents as high as 10,000. There is a smaller number in New Zealand. The International Sufi Movement has also continued to grow in numbers and popularity and another of Inayat's sons, Hidayat Inayat Khan (b. 1917) took on the leadership in 1988. The movement's headquarters are located at The Hague under the guidance of Dr H.J. Witteveen, a Dutchman initiated in 1921 and known as Murshid Karimbakhsh. The International Sufi Movement has three major objectives:

1. To realize and spread the knowledge of Unity, the religion of love and wisdom, so that the bias of faiths and beliefs may of itself fall away, the human heart may overflow with love, and all hatred caused by distinctions and differences may be rooted out.

2. To discover the light and power latent in man, the secret of all religion, the power of mysticism and the essence of philosophy, without interfering with customs and beliefs.

3. To help to bring the world's two opposite poles, East and West, close together by the interchange of thought and ideals; that the universal brotherhood may form of itself and may meet with persons beyond the narrow national and racial boundaries.

Present Practice

The International Sufi Movement has five major concerns: The Brotherhood/Sisterhood Activity, Universal Worship, the School of Inner Culture or Esoteric Activity, Spiritual Healing and Symbology.

l. The Brotherhood/Sisterhood Activity stresses that 'there is one human Brotherhood and Sisterhood which unites all the children of earth in the Fatherhood of God'. Each Sufi devotee can measure his or her progress by the extent to which he or she has developed the spirit of brotherhood. Sufism stresses that this spirit of brotherhood, a theme shared by the entire world's religions, is needed more than ever before in the history of the world. In words with an echo of US President John F. Kennedy (1917–63), Hidayat Inayat Khan urges: 'Let us stop wondering what others could do for us, but rather ask ourselves what we could do for others.'

2. The Universal Worship activity was introduced by Hazrat Inayat Khan in a major ceremony in London in May 1921. It is the logical outworking of the Sufi concept of brotherhood and sisterhood and is the school where Sufis seek to learn the lesson of tolerance. Devotees

must avoid saying, 'Your religion is worse and my religion is better.' Instead they should worship together with those of other beliefs and commitments.

3. The Inner School focuses on the inner culture of the soul with the aim of helping each individual to realize his or her true self. This is a process which begins with initiation and then leads on to a gradual introduction to the teachings of Hazrat Inayat Khan. The symbol of the Sufi Movement is the heart with wings. This depicts the fact that the heart stands between the soul and the body, a medium between the spirit and matter. The wings are a symbolic reminder that there is always the potential for upward spiritual progress. Sufism aims to loosen the ties which bind initiates to the material world and enable them to reach heavenward.

4. Spiritual healing is an important aspect of Sufism. Hazrat Inayat Khan taught that the power to heal flows through the individual who is divested of the self. Such a person, according to Inayat, 'realizes that the body, which is the temple of God, should be a fitting habitation for its heavenly guest'. Inayat saw illness as 'nothing but inharmony', maintaining that the secret of health 'lies in harmony'. Sufi healing also utilizes herbal and holistic medical practice.

5. The School of Symbology seeks to deepen the awareness of the importance of symbols in daily life. In order to appreciate symbols more fully, the mind needs to be cleared of unwanted thoughts and regrets. The devotee needs to learn to see beyond the symbol to the divine presence which lies behind. Such symbols may be found

in nature or in the world's great religious traditions.
Sacred dance forms an important part of Sufi symbology
by helping to generate mystical experience.

In Sufism the priesthood has no exalted status. It exists only to
take the services and give pastoral support. There is no
distinction between men and women and in a more general
sense every Sufi man and woman is a priest, preacher and
teacher to every person they encounter. Praise and prayer form
a very important part of Sufi spirituality. Praise is the opening of
the heart to divine beauty of the creation. Prayer, which
expresses gratitude for the goodness of God, can be either silent
or aloud.

33.   The Theosophical Movement

Origins

Theosophy means 'wisdom of god'. Theosophy is the wisdom underlying all religions when they are stripped of accretions and superstitions. The modern Theosophical Movement was established by Helena Blavatsky (1831–91) and Henry Steel Olcott (1832–1907). Helena Petrovna von Hahn was born into a well-connected family in Yekaterinoslav (now Dnepropetrovsk, Ukraine). At the age of seventeen she married a considerably older man, General Nicephore Blavatsky. Their union proved to be unhappy and they separated after only a few months. Madame Blavatsky, who had a keen interest in the occult, travelled widely in the East, including Tibet, and in 1873 went to the USA, where she met Colonel Olcott at a mediumistic display of table-turning and spirit knockings by the Fox sisters, Margaret, Catherine and Katie. Together Olcott and Blavatsky founded the Theosophical Society in New York City in 1875. In 1879 Blavatsky and Olcott left the USA for India and established the movement's international headquarters where they still remain today at Adya, near Madras.

After having been investigated for fraud, Blavatsky left India and travelled extensively in Europe. She eventually settled in London, where she continued writing and produced *The Secret*

Doctrine (1888) and *The Voice of Silence* (1889). She engaged in various forms of Spiritualism and large crowds sometimes attended her séances. At one point her practices were investigated by the British Society for Psychical Research and she was declared to be a fraudulent medium. She died on 8 May 1891.

Following the death of Olcott, the charismatic Annie Besant (1847–1933) became the society's president and remained in post until her death. Its worldwide membership grew under her from 15,000 to a peak of over 40,000 in 1929. Her publications are felt by many to represent the clearest expressions of Theosophy. The Theosophical Society in England has three stated objectives:

1. **To form a nucleus of the universal brotherhood of humanity without distinction of race, creed, sex, caste or colour.**
2. **To encourage the study of comparative religion, philosophy and science.**
3. **To investigate unexplained laws of nature and the powers latent in man.**

These core aims, which derive from Madame Blavatsky's *Key to Philosophy* (1889), have remained unchanged to the present time.

Core Beliefs

● There is a uniting 'red thread', which is shared by all religions.
● God is the impersonal source of all things and is reflected in all things.
● Jesus is held to be one of many great religious teachers and not regarded as divine.

- Human beings are an extension of God. God is latent in all humanity.
- Human beings are essentially soul. The body is simply a garment, worn for a time and then discarded.
- By one's actions (*karma*) an individual can either go forwards or backwards on the wheel of reincarnation. The ultimate goal is to progress upwards and come to occupy a celestial body.
- Death is a recurring event in an endless life.
- Salvation is a conscious awareness of the deep hidden knowledge/divine nature which resides in every human being.
- There is no hell.

Recent Developments

A number of very influential and creative people have been attracted to Theosophy, including the playwright Oscar Wilde (1854–1900), the poet W.B. Yeats (1865–1939), the author George Bernard Shaw (1856–1950), the inventor Thomas Edison (1847–1931) and artists Wassily Kandinsky (1866–1944), Piet Mondrian (1872–1944) and Paul Klee (1879–1940). The movement has played a major role in promoting Buddhism and Hinduism among the higher social strata of the nations of the West. Whilst it is the case that Theosophy is not making the impact it once did, it is a fact that many contemporary esoteric movements have built on elements of its teaching. A number of New Age concepts, including the practice of channelling, also draw on theosophy. No accurate reports of membership are kept, but academic sources estimate the number of current adherents to be in the region of 40,000 worldwide, with 5,000 in the USA.

Present Practice

The Theosophical Society holds to the stated core beliefs, but acceptance of them is not a requirement of membership of the society. All that is required is a commitment to the three stated objectives. The society is non-sectarian and non-political and open to all people regardless of race, nationality, class, creed or gender. 'What is a theosophist?' In answering the question, Madame Blavatsky wrote: 'One need not necessarily recognize the existence of any special god or deity. One need but worship the spirit of living nature and try to identify oneself with it.' Theosophy has no set rituals, and meetings most often consist of talks and discussion or the study of a book. In addition, there are workshops and summer schools.

34.   Transcendental Meditation

Origins

Transcendental Meditation was first devised and taught by the Maharishi Mahesh Yogi in 1957. Although it claims to be a purely scientific technique, it has strong Hindu roots. Its great appeal is that it is not demanding in terms of time and can easily be learned by anyone, regardless of his or her age or educational background. Furthermore, it requires no special belief, lifestyle or diet.

The Maharishi Mahesh Yogi was born Mahesh Prasad Warma at Jabalpur, India (possibly 1917). He studied Physics at the University of Allahabad and graduated in 1940. Following this he spent the next thirteen years in seclusion studying under Swami Brahmananda Saraswati (1869–1953), usually known as Guru Dev, at Jyotir Monastery in Badarinath. After Guru Dev's death Mahesh spent two more years in study before presenting his teachings to the world. Transcendental Meditation (TM) is the most prominent aspect of his wider Vedic Science and Technology.

In 1958 Mahesh assumed the title 'Maharishi' (Great Seer), when he founded his worldwide Spiritual Regeneration Movement in Madras. By 1959 he had begun to influence the USA, a fact that became apparent with the founding of the

Maharishi International University in Iowa in 1971. He had travelled to London in 1960, but what really brought the movement to the attention of the British public was the 1968 visit of the Beatles to India to learn from him.

In 1972 he inaugurated his World Plan to provide instruction across the globe in 'The Science of Consciousness, the Science of Creative Intelligence'. The scheme involved the training of 2,000 teachers of this science. In 1975 the Maharishi declared that he had discovered the full potential of Natural Law and he went on to announce the 'Dawn of the Age of Enlightenment' to some 30 million viewers on *The Merv Griffin Show*, with Griffin himself announcing that he had already been benefiting for some time from practising TM with encouragement from Clint Eastwood.

Core Beliefs

Transcendental Meditation is rooted in the Hindu tradition and therefore shares a number of its major beliefs:
● the cycle of birth, death and rebirth.
● recognition of the Hindu gods.
● the importance of the Vedic texts.

Recent Developments

A notable feature of the Maharishi's 'Science of Consciousness' has been the practice of yogic flying, which began in 1976. The first conference of 7,000 yogic flyers took place at Fairfield, Iowa, USA in 1984. In 1988 the Maharishi published his *Master Plan to Create Heaven on Earth* and formed a new political party, The

Natural Law Party, with the specific aim of influencing governments with his 'Supreme Political Science'. He followed this in 1997 with the establishment of his 'Global Administration through Natural Law' with twelve 'Time Zone Capitals' around the world. The 1990s also witnessed the Maharishi's entry into British politics when The Natural Law party first began to put up candidates in the local, European and national elections.

By the beginning of the twenty-first century the number of teachers across the globe providing instruction in 'The Science of Consciousness, the Science of Creative Intelligence' was reported to have reached 40,000. The movement claims that over 4 million people around the world practise Transcendental Meditation, of whom about 160,000 are located in Britain.

Present Practice

The Maharishi and his followers assert that TM is not a religion but a scientific, non-religious technique to bring about better levels of health and wholeness. There is, however, no doubt that it has strong roots in Hinduism. Its basic principles are grounded in the Vedic scriptures. When individuals are initiated into the movement, the ceremony requires them to stand in front of a picture of Guru Dev and to present an offering of fruit, flowers and a handkerchief during a time of devotional singing or *puja* (reverence, worship). The ritual also involves invocations to Lord Narayana and to Brahma the Creator and bowing down before Guru Dev. Once the *puja* is completed, initiates receive their own personal mantra that is selected on the basis of their sex and age. The mantra is a verbal formula or sound that is constantly repeated silently (that is, the individual thinks the sound) or chanted out aloud. Devotees must then meditate using this mantra for fifteen to twenty minutes each morning and evening. This enables him or her to connect the outer field of activity with the inner self, resulting in a heightened sense of consciousness and a deep sense of relaxation, alertness and peace. TM also claims to reduce anxiety and depression and increase intelligence and creativity. Against these views, some recent surveys have claimed that TM practitioners have encountered a range of negative side effects, including panic, loss of motivation and feelings of guilt, apprehension and despair. Those who wish to develop TM to a higher level can go on to more advanced techniques such as yogic flying, which is achieved by perfect mind-body coordination.

35.   The Unification Church

Origins

The Unification Church (recently renamed the Family Federation for World Peace and Unification, FFWPU) is one of many organizations founded by Sun Myung Moon, who was born in the village of Cheong-Ju in what is now North Korea on 6 January 1920. His parents became committed members of the Presbyterian Church when he was ten years old. According to Unification sources, on Easter Sunday 1936 he received a vision in which Jesus appeared to him. Moon relates that he was asked to complete the mission that Jesus had been unable to achieve. Jesus had accomplished the work of spiritual redemption, but his efforts to bring about humankind's physical redemption had been prevented on account of his arrest and death on the cross.

In 1941 Moon went to Waseda University in Japan to study engineering. In 1943 he returned to Korea and worked for a construction company. The period immediately following the end of the war was a time of great religious expectancy in Korea and Sun Myung Moon decided to become a full-time preacher. In 1943 he married Sun Kil Choi, a deeply committed Christian woman. Shortly after the birth of their first son, Moon stated that he had received a revelation that he was to go to the North Korean city of Pyongyang. Leaving his wife and child behind,

Moon set off in November 1952. The separation and the demands of being a preacher's wife proved to be too much for Sun Kil Choi and she divorced him. It should be noted, however, that both Sun Kil Choi and their son subsequently became members of the Unification Church.

Moon was dissatisfied with the Presbyterian Church, from which he had been expelled in 1948 for unorthodox doctrinal views, with the result that while he was in North Korea he founded Kwang-ya, an independent Christian church with a strongly charismatic ethos. In 1954 Moon returned to Seoul and founded The Holy Spirit Association for the Unification of World Christianity, which later became known as The Unification Church. The following year the Korean edition of Moon's most significant writing, *The Divine Principle*, was published. Its central message is that Jesus, who was not virgin born, failed in his mission to establish the perfect family because he never married. Soon after the publication of *The Divine Principle*, Moon received a prison sentence that he claimed was on account of his opposition to communism. Other accusations were made against him at the time, but none were ever substantiated. Since Moon saw his role as to finish the mission that Jesus failed to complete, he remarried in 1960. His new wife, Hak Ja Han, was an eighteen-year-old member of the church. The marriage was referred to as 'the marriage of the lamb'. Moon and Hak Ja Han are held to be the 'true parents' who are able through the blessing ceremony to bring people into the family of God.

In 1958 the first Unification Church missionary, Sang Ik-Choi, was sent out to Japan where Moon's new organization grew rapidly. Other missionaries were commissioned to serve in the USA, where the Oakland Family in California became a very important outreach centre. In 1973 'crusade' teams were sent to travel to every state of the USA and the Reverend Moon gave speeches in each state. In 1980 the USA headquarters were moved to New York and Moses Durst, one of the early Oakland missionaries, became the movement's national president.

The recruitment methods of the various US groups differed a good deal. The Oakland group made little mention of Sun Myung Moon and invited people off the streets to weekend retreats and conferences, while the New York practice was to teach the theology of the *Divine Principle*. In the 1980s frequent charges of brainwashing were made against the Unification Church, but careful scrutiny revealed that never more than 10 per cent of those who attended the seminars and conferences actually joined the church. Professor Eileen Barker of London University in her researches in the UK found that only two out of every hundred who attended seminars eventually became members of the church.

Moon had successfully invested in a number of business and publishing ventures and his strong stand against communism brought him some degree of acclaim in the West. In 1972 he purchased an estate in upstate New York that was then valued at $850,000 and Moon and his wife subsequently took up residence there. This relocation marked a decisive step forward and the movement began to expand rapidly. Moon needed immediate sums of money to fund his projected recruitment drive and business expansion plans. To this end he devised the concept of mobile fundraising teams. These groups of largely enthusiastic young people engaged in extensive street campaigns in every US state selling flowers, sweets, magazines and candles or merely asking for money for social projects. Jacqui Williams, a British member of the church until 1982, reported in her autobiography that she sometimes made $3,500 in a month.

Carlo Zaccarelli, still a member, recalls averaging $80 a day in the early 1980s.

What many felt to be the church's strongly right-wing political sympathies reached a climax in 1974 with public support for Richard Nixon. Moon had shared a public platform with Nixon and hoped the American people would forgive the president for his part in the Watergate scandal and remain committed to his fight against world communism.

In the 1980s Moon was found guilty of tax evasion by the US fiscal administration. In short, it was alleged, he had failed to include a sum of the order of $112,000 in his personal tax return. Other Unification sources claimed it was as little as $7,000. The fact remains that the precise sum that was disputed was relatively small when set against the church's income that ran into millions of dollars. Nevertheless, Moon was sentenced to eighteen months in prison and began his sentence on 13 May 1984. His term was reduced by five months for good conduct. The imprisonment brought a storm of protest from many quarters that were focused on the issue of religious freedom. One Baptist pastor commented: 'The Government is trying to get him off the streets.' On Moon's release, the Reverend Jerry Falwell and other national leaders of both conservative and liberal views held a press conference in his support. Their backing made a significant impact in helping to change the general public's view of the Unification Church.

Core Beliefs

● The Bible is insufficient and *The Divine Principle* is necessary to 'shed new light'.

- God is invisible and has a dual nature that embraces positive and negative, masculine and feminine, love and beauty.
- God's divine purpose is to establish the perfect family.
- Original sin was brought about because the first man and the first woman united sexually before they had received God's 'blessing'.
- By his life and death on the cross Jesus, the Second Adam, achieved spiritual salvation but was unable to accomplish the work of physical salvation.
- Jesus may be understood to be God's second self, but he is not God himself.
- Because Jesus failed in his mission, a Third Adam, the Lord of the Second Advent, is needed to come and complete the work of physical salvation. 'The Lord of the Second Advent will not come on the clouds... he will be born on earth in the flesh.'
- The Reverend Sun Myung Moon is the Lord of the Second Advent and he and his second wife, Hak Ja Han, are the 'True Parents'. Couples are grafted into the family by receiving their 'true blessing' in one of the specially organized blessing ceremonies.
- 'Korea should be the nation that can receive the Lord of the Second Advent.'
- 'The Korean people will become the third Israel, God's elect.'

Recent Developments

Since the 1980s the character and ethos of the Unification Church has changed a good deal. Since 1989 and the collapse of the Berlin Wall its hostility to communism has been replaced by a focus on peace, with many peace conferences organized around the world. This is most obviously visible in Mrs Moon's speaking tours on behalf of the Women's Federation for World Peace. In July 1993 she addressed the US Congress on this theme and in September of the same year she went on to speak to representatives of the General Assembly of the United Nations.

By the mid-1990s the church had shifted its focus of activity from North to South America, where it invested $25 million in the purchase of 7.5 million acres of land in various parts of the continent. This project known as the New Hope East Garden includes land reclamation and regeneration, fish farming and agricultural research.

As Moon grows older, the matter of his succession has become a matter of increasing importance. In July 1998 Moon's third son, Hyun Jin Moon, was inaugurated as vice-president of the Family Federation for World Peace and Unification.

The intensity of the movement's earlier recruitment activities has subsided and its energies are largely spent in organizing inter-religious peace conferences, where leaders of the major world faiths come together to discuss ways in which they can bring about reconciliation and work together. In the UK the Unification Church has just a few hundred members. There are area churches with pastors in London, where there are four congregations, Birmingham, Manchester and the West Country, centred on Bristol and Bath. There is also a congregation in Scotland. In Australia there are currently eight centres with approximately 300 members. The Unification movement remains active in the USA and the Far East. The Unification Church is strongest in Japan and Korea and parts of South America. Its current membership is reckoned to be of the order of 250,000 worldwide. North American membership was estimated at 10,000 in 2003 with less than a thousand in the UK.

Present Practice

As with most other churches, the Unification Church has not been without its public relations difficulties. Nansook Hong, the wife of Moon's eldest son, Hyo Jin, divorced him in 1998 citing many years of drug use and violent and adulterous behaviour. This did not sit well with Moon's agenda to establish the perfect family. To their credit Moon and his wife readily admitted to their failure and it has to be recognized that at the time of their children's growing years they were pursuing a punishing schedule of world travel and organization.

The ceremony for which the Unification Church is most renowned is the mass public wedding. At these occasions couples already married in other services or 'matched' by the Reverend Moon share a cup of consecrated wine in a pledge that theirs is an eternal union. Both women and men are free to refuse the choice which is made for them and attend another matching ceremony. The first mass wedding ceremony took place in Korea in 1970, when the Reverend and Mrs Moon 'blessed' 777 couples. A similar event took place in 1975 at Seoul when 1,800 couples exchanged vows. The numbers at subsequent ceremonies have continued to expand hugely. This was powerfully demonstrated on 13 June 1998 when a ceremony took place at Madison Square Garden in New York City that was reported to include 120 million couples worldwide. Latterly, the matching of couples has been increasingly delegated to the senior members of the church's hierarchy. Not all Unificationists are blessed in a mass ceremony. It can be just one couple.

Much of Unification Church spirituality is centred on the home. Each Sunday members gather at 5 a.m. and recite 'the pledge', which is a commitment to 'God and True Parents' and to 'establish the original ideal of creation, the kingdom of God on Earth and in Heaven'. The pledge is also made on a number of holy days at 7 a.m., when members dress in white holy robes before an offering table on which there is a photograph of the Reverend and Mrs Moon. Sunday worship services are quite similar in ethos to many standard Free Church services with songs, prayers, readings from the Bible and *The Divine Principle* and a sermon. The church does not practise baptism, although water is sometimes sprinkled at the birth ceremony that takes place eight days after the birth.

An important aspect of Unification spirituality is the paying of indemnities. These are basically penances or disciplines which individuals pay in order to free themselves from Satan's grip, particularly when they are conscious of having done wrong of any kind. In this way members renew their relationship with God.

The church has undoubtedly changed in its ethos over the years and its successful business ventures in pharmaceuticals, manufacturing and military equipment have made it increasingly wealthy. It should be noted that in the 1970s all Korean factories, the Unification Church factories included, were required to contribute to the government's military armament programme. The movement's other holdings included *The New York City Tribune* and *The Washington Times*, which was created in 1982. *The Tribune* was closed down in the late 1980s, but *The Times* continues to offer a firmly conservative, pro-Republican alternative to *The Washington Post*. Some of the church's businesses have raised considerable funds that have obviated the need for vigorous recruitment and street fundraisers.

36. The Worldwide Church of God

Origins

The Worldwide Church of God was founded in 1933 by Herbert W. Armstrong (1892–1986), who was born of Quaker parents in Des Moines, Iowa. In his early years Armstrong pursued a career in the advertising world, first in his home town and then in Chicago, where he dreamed of making a fortune. In 1917 he married his third cousin, Loma Dillon, in a Baptist church. Following the depression of 1920, Armstrong moved his young family to Salem, Oregon, where in the middle of a desperate financial situation his wife became fanatically attached to Seventh-day Adventist beliefs, including the necessity of worshipping on the sabbath as opposed to Sunday. Armstrong eventually became convinced by Loma's arguments and submitted to baptism by immersion at the hands of a local Baptist minister.

In 1928 he began preaching and in 1931 he was ordained into the ministry of the Church of God (Seventh Day). Two years later he broke with the church and established his own ministry, which developed into The Radio Church of God in Eugene, Oregon, in 1934, and later became known as The World of Tomorrow radio ministry. In that same year he published the first issue of *The Plain Truth* magazine with 106 subscribers.

Events moved quickly and in 1947 Ambassador College was founded as a liberal arts establishment in Pasadena, California, the auditorium costing more than $11 million. A further major step forward came in 1953 when Armstrong began broadcasting into Europe from Radio Luxembourg. The high standard of his programmes and the well-written articles in *The Plain Truth*, many of which were on issues of the environment, morality and culture, were enormously appealing to many people. The current name, the Worldwide Church of God, was adopted in 1968. At the height of Armstrong's fame the magazine reached a circulation peak of 5,813,000 in 1988.

It was not always apparent from his publications that Armstrong was rigidly attached to several doctrines, some derived from Seventh-day Adventism and Old Testament Judaism, which were not shared by mainstream Christian churches. This enabled him to retain a fairly widespread appeal. The Worldwide Church of God's distinctive teachings included the strict observance of the Saturday sabbath, the keeping of Jewish festivals, the requirement to eat only the clean meats listed in Leviticus 11 and the rejection of the traditional doctrines of salvation, heaven and hell. Moreover, a key part of Armstrong's theology was his British Israelite conviction that the white Anglo-Saxon Protestants of the USA and Britain were the 'pure' descendants of ancient Israel and God's true people on earth.

As the movement grew, the membership was increasingly controlled by the church's leadership, who laid down strict regulations on such matters as food, dress and dating. Members were also required to give up to 30 per cent of their income.

Among those who rose to prominence in the movement was Armstrong's youngest child, Garner Ted Armstrong (1930–2003), who like his father was a gifted and persuasive preacher. He began broadcasting in 1955, the year of his ordination. Garner Ted had dreamed in his youth of becoming a nightclub celebrity. After a period of teenage rebellion and a term of service in the navy he studied at Ambassador College, where he became convinced that 'Dad's religion was… the religion of Jesus.' He graduated with bachelor's, master's and doctorate degrees.

In 1957 Garner Ted took over the weekly *World of Tomorrow* show from his father and it has been estimated that his voice was eventually heard on more than 300 radio stations on every continent. In addition, by the 1970s he was seen by millions on more than 160 US television stations. While still only in his early thirties, Armstrong also became the executive vice-president of the church, an executive of *The Plain Truth* and president of Ambassador College. The expanding popularity of 'Armstrongism' facilitated further developments. In 1960 a second Ambassador College was opened in Bricket Wood, England – although it closed in 1976 – and a third was established at Big Sandy, Texas, in 1964.

A period of intense controversy began in 1972, the year for which Herbert Armstrong had prophesied that the Worldwide Church of God would be raptured and transplanted into the desert city of Petra in Jordan. Not only did the prophecy fail to materialize, but Garner Ted had to be removed from broadcasting, the church declaring that he was 'in the bonds of Satan'. According to one report, he had struggled with adultery over a nineteen-year period and had also been involved in excessive gambling in Las Vegas. Herbert Armstrong was lenient towards his son's immoral behaviour and in 1973 named him as his successor. However, the final break came in 1978 when Garner Ted attempted to take over the entire movement while his father was ill.

The removal of Garner Ted left a major hole in the life of the church that had disastrous consequences. It resulted in the loss of his huge influence on hundreds of radio and television stations; and gone too were his many appealing and attractive magazine articles. Garner Ted immediately sought to recover his personal losses by moving to Tyler, Texas, where he founded his own organization, the Church of God International, which continued to proclaim his father's teachings. Soon he was back on the airwaves too and he launched *Twentieth Century Watch* to rival his father's *The Plain Truth*. The church grew rapidly and by the early 1980s its income was approaching the $1 million mark. However, in 1995 there was a major setback when Armstrong was caught on a hidden camera soliciting sex from a masseuse in Tyler. He was removed from his church, but continued to broadcast through The Garner Ted Armstrong Evangelical Association. In 1998 he founded yet another church, The Intercontinental Church of God. He was president of both organizations when he died in September 2003.

Despite having excommunicated his son for immoral behaviour, Herbert Armstrong himself was not free of personal scandal. He was a known, profligate spender on entertainment and like Garner Ted frequently travelled on church-provided private jets. He had a fashionable home in Pasadena, a country estate in Texas and a Victorian house on the outskirts of London. In 1977, following Loma's death, he married a former switchboard operator, Ramona Martin, a divorcee forty-six years his junior. This was particularly controversial because Armstrong had been publicly adamant against divorce. To compound the matter, he divorced her against her wishes in 1984. He died less than two years later at the age of ninety-three amid allegations that he had abused his younger daughter

Dorothy in her childhood years and that he had siphoned off huge sums of the church's money for his private use. In consequence of this and declining membership the church found it necessary to sell a major part of Ambassador College's campus in Pasadena, California.

Core Beliefs

The following were the main tenets of Armstrong's theology:

- The Bible is a coded book, not intended to be understood until the twentieth century.
- God is not a Trinity and the Eternal Father and Jesus Christ are two separate persons.
- Jesus alone of all humans has so far been saved and baptism is an essential ordinance for salvation.
- Salvation will be accomplished when Jesus Christ returns to earth. Those who die without Christ will have an opportunity to commit their lives to him during his rule on earth in the millennium that is a period of bliss at the end of the world.
- Members of the WCG will become gods.
- The apocalypse will begin in 1936. (Later the date was set for 1943, then 1972; then it was postponed indefinitely.)
- The white Anglo-Saxon Protestants of America and Britain are the 'pure' descendants of the ten lost tribes of ancient Israel.
- Saturday is to be observed as the sabbath day for worship.
- Only the clean meats listed in Leviticus 11 are to be eaten.
- Laws which were binding on Old Testament Jews continue to be binding on Christians.

Recent Developments

Despite the difficulties surrounding his later years Herbert Armstrong's organization experienced something of an upturn. His broadcasts and membership both expanded and he continued to appear on the media until his death, at which time the leadership passed to Joseph W. Tkach (1927–95), a former aircraft factory foreman from Chicago, who began the process of doctrinal change which eventually resulted in the church returning to more orthodox Christian doctrines. Tkach recognized that some of Armstrong's beliefs had no biblical foundation. In 1988 Tkach taught that it was permissible to go to doctors, take medicines, observe birthdays and wear cosmetics. In 1991 the doctrine that men would one day be gods was repudiated and it was recognized that the Holy Spirit was part of the godhead. A new interpretation of the ten tribes of Israel was also given. In 1993 the church accepted the doctrine of the Trinity In 1994 the observance of a strictly-kept Saturday sabbath, which involved devoting extra time to prayer, Bible study and meditation and avoiding activities such as hunting, fishing, golfing, swimming and going to the cinema, was abandoned. Tkach also revoked the keeping of other Old Covenant laws regarding tithing and the eating of meat. In consequence of having adopted more mainstream Christian teachings, the WCG incurred considerable loss of members and revenue and was forced to sell real estate to offset its debts.

In 1995 Tkach died and the board of directors honoured his request by appointing his son, Joseph Jr (b. 1951), as his successor. The church currently reports 60,000 members worldwide, half of them in the USA.

Present Practice

The Worldwide Church of God has come to be identified largely with Christian orthodoxy, although some have expressed concerns that it still holds to a modified universalist view of salvation.

37.   New Age Religion

Origins

'New Age' has become very much an umbrella term, making it a phenomenon that is not easy to define. It does, however, have a number of generally agreed characteristics. All life is believed to be the manifestation of one god or divine spirit who is present in everything (sometimes termed pantheistic monism). It means that all living things are believed to be potentially divine, including humanity, and leads logically to a second New Age preoccupation, namely that of self-realization, realizing one's individual potential and getting in touch with one's divinity. This in turn has resulted in the adoption of a wide variety of rituals and techniques, all of which are aimed at heightening the individual's self-awareness and enabling him or her to get into touch with the inner spirit. New Agers believe that this heightened self-awareness is the way to the New Age, which is also the 'Age of Aquarius', a 2,000-year period of supreme religious awakening for humanity, marked by peace, prosperity, happiness and enlightenment. This era is believed to have begun in the 1960s with the passing of the Judaeo-Christian age, the 'Age of Pisces', although many regard the New Age as not having officially commenced until the early 1970s. The major means of achieving these qualities are the rejection of materialism, becoming more sociable, and being attuned to the creation.

Since New Agers believe that God, the universal spirit, pervades all of creation, it is logical for them to invest it with divine status. Most of their number honour the earth as the goddess Gaia. For this reason the New Age movement is strongly linked with ecological programmes, environmental concerns and anti-pollution projects.

The monism of the New Age means that all of creation and the entire human race are not merely linked but bound together in a cosmic unity. As a consequence New Agers strongly embrace multicultural initiatives and multicultural and multi-ethnic integration (and in Britain, for the most part, are strong advocates of European unity). Because its spiritualities value and emphasize the significance of the feminine, the New Age movement has added considerably to the feminist cause and the improved status of women. The New Age is firmly tolerant of all the major world faiths, as well as the teaching and practices of many smaller sectarian offshoots. David Spangler (b. 1945), a prominent New Age author, commented on this matter as follows: 'There is an encounter going on between all the great faith traditions. Out of that encounter comes a deeper sense of what is our common spirituality.'

The ultimate goal for those who embrace the New Age is the capacity to express one's higher self, which will result in the ability to express unconditional love. All of the wide range of occult practice, meditations, yoga and therapies are directed towards this end. The New Age has a particular appeal to those who have become disillusioned with the traditional, mainstream, denominational churches, since it has no creeds, clergy or institutional hierarchical administration.

The roots of the New Age movement run back into the eighteenth century and more particularly the nineteenth century, when Hinduism and other Eastern religions began to be introduced into the West. Transcendentalism, spiritualism and Theosophy all contributed to new ways of thinking and have been described as 'the seedbed of the New Age'. The modern Theosophical Movement was established in New York City in 1875 by Helena Blavatsky together with Colonel Olcott and others (*see The Theosophical Movement). Blavatsky drew on Hindu mystical traditions and the Jewish *Kabbalah*, a system of ancient mystical knowledge compiled by Moses de Leon in the thirteenth century. Madame Blavatsky was an active medium and professed to receive many of her teachings from the 'Ancient Masters' or Adepts through séances. These were eventually published as *The Secret Doctrine* (1888). An influential and later associate of Theosophy was Alice A. Bailey (1880–1949). Departing from the evangelical Christian environment of her earlier days, from the 1920s she claimed to receive revelations from Djwal Khul, a hidden adept or 'Master of the Wisdom' in Tibet. Many of his channelled teachings she committed to print, as in *A Treatise on Cosmic Fire* and *Discipleship in the New Age*. These and others of Alice Bailey's writings have been influential New Age texts.

Bailey, it should be noted, shared the strongly anti-Semitic views of Blavatsky. For example, Bailey wrote of the Jews as 'the world's greatest problem', claiming that their separateness militated against universal human unity. Among many other anti-Semitic comments, Bailey wrote in her *Unfinished Autobiography*: 'Jews frequently lower the atmosphere of any district in which they reside.' In *Esoteric Healing* she wrote: 'The Jew has never grasped the love of God. The God of the Jews is possessive and greedy, Jehovah is not God.' In *Rays and Initiations* she said: 'The Jews are the reincarnation of spiritual failures or residues from another planet.' It should be stressed that New Agers as a whole are not anti-Semitic and many would be profoundly shocked by these expressions of the Jews as an inferior race.

Core Beliefs

Common beliefs, not shared in every case by all groups, are:

- Monism (the belief that every diverse thing in the world has its origin in a single source).
- Pantheism or the belief that 'all is one and all is God'; God is therefore not a person or a personal creator but 'the Force'.
- Humanity's immortal divinity; the realization of that divinity being the goal for every human being; 'Everyone is God' (Shirley MacLaine).
- Reincarnation based on the concept of *karma* (actions and consequences), with good karma moving individuals towards a higher state.
- The ultimate restoration to wholeness of the creation, which is a living being, Gaia, with men and women discovering new powers within themselves that will be released into the earth to right ecological imbalances.
- The disappearance of boundaries leading to the world becoming a global family.
- One universal religion (the belief that all the different religions in the world are alternate paths to the same end).

Recent Developments

In recent times, when endorsement by celebrities has drawn the interest of the public to many causes, the New Age has been popularized by the actress Shirley MacLaine (b. 1934), whose autobiography *Out On a Limb* (1983) was a hugely influential bestseller.

There are a number of centres and festivals that are important to New Age practitioners. Britain's oldest New Age centre is the Findhorn Community, founded by Peter and Eileen Caddy in 1962 in a small village on the Moray Firth, just east of Inverness. Of particular significance is the Findhorn Garden, created by Peter Caddy (1917–94) following instructions that Eileen received from the 'devas' or nature spirits, with most workshops taking place in the splendid Universal Hall, a pentagonal building on a site where many ley lines are said to converge. Since the 1960s Glastonbury has also been regarded as particularly important, since it is believed to be the 'heart *chakra*' of the earth and a communication point for alien contact. Popular centres in the USA include the Renaissance Community in Massachusetts, the Lama Foundation in New Mexico and the Esalen Institute in California, which was founded in 1962 by two psychology graduates, Michael Murphy and Richard Price, and dedicated to the 'exploration of human potential'. Esalen is situated in the Santa Lucia Mountains and named after the Esalen tribe that once inhabited the area.

One of the most celebrated demonstrations took place on 16–17 August 1987. More than 80 million New Agers across the globe unified themselves in what was the largest ever mass meditation in history. Described as the 'Harmonic Convergence', it was planned and led by 144,000 shamans, witches, and witch doctors. Their aim was to release spiritual forces that would bring about their desire for 'a one world religion and a one world government'.

As has been noted, the New Age is a very broad-based movement that embraces and networks other organizations into 'The Plan' for 'The New World Order'. Among those with which it has strong links are Share International and the Tara Centre, both headed by Benjamin Creme; Whole Earth Catalogues; the Lucis Trust, who publish Alice Bailey's writings; and the Lorian Association, headed by David Spangler. Also associated are a number of neo-pagan societies, green and nature religionists and occult and psychic groups such as the Theosophical Society. New Age practices have a very wide-ranging appeal. In recent times many of these groups have both drawn on New Age practices and in turn contributed some of their ideas, therapies and rituals.

The New Age or 'Age of Aquarius' will only become visible when there is a sufficient 'critical mass' of initiates or 'enlightened ones' active in the world to assert the end of the 'Age of Pisces', which is believed to have ushered in the 'Christian era'. Conservative Christians, Orthodox and Zionist Jews and fundamentalist Muslims are seen as creating a resistance to humankind's achieving worldwide unity.

Present Practice

In seeking to reach the 'higher self' New Agers engage in a whole range of practices that are drawn from a wide variety of sources, including the Christian tradition. All are essentially forms of self-love and include various kinds of meditation, yoga, holistic medicine and divination. Meditation embraces the use of mantra (repetitive chants), breath meditation that focuses the mind through breathing exercises, and 'mindfulness' in which the mind is made to focus on the body. Yoga (Sanskrit for 'to join, to unite') is a series of body movements and exercises designed to unite the body and mind. Holistic medicine addresses the needs of the whole person: body, mind and spirit. It advocates a wide range of techniques including aromatherapy, homeopathy, massage, acupuncture, herbalism, colour therapy, crystal healing and *t'ai chi*. All of these therapies make full use of nature including stones, plants, leaves, herbs, ointments and oils. Japanese Reiki healing, which is administered with the laying on of hands, is widely practised. Reiki is compounded of two Japanese characters, *rei* meaning 'universal wisdom' and *ki* meaning 'life force energy'. This energy is believed to flow through every person and New Age practitioners simply channel it to the person who is in need of healing or strength. New Agers believe the spirit of 'Mother Earth' is present in every aspect of the creation and that there is particular power in crystals. For example, rose quartz is said to be a generally useful and particularly helpful to those with emotional pain. Crystal therapy can involve holding crystals in the palm of the hand or placing them on particular parts of the body or at energy points (*chakras*). In very general terms, treatments involving surgery and artificial drugs are avoided where possible.

There are New Agers who value various forms of divination, including tarot reading, astrology and palmistry. Some New Age writers do not regard Satan as a symbol of evil. They believe that he has been misunderstood and misrepresented by Jews and Christians alike. New Agers honour him as Lucifer or the bearer of light, as the ultimate-being turned god. David Spangler, for instance, conflates Lucifer with Christ in his book *Reflections of the Christ* (1978): 'Christ is the same force as Lucifer [...]. Lucifer prepares us for Christhood [...]. Lucifer works within each of us to bring us to wholeness, and as we move into a new age [...] each of us in some way is brought to that point which I term the Luciferic initiation [...] that [...] is an initiation into the New Age.' Lucifer is believed to be the one who has inspired and sustained all the outstanding representatives of the human race. His sacred number is held to be 666 and is used, whenever the occasion arises, to hasten his appearance.

New Agers celebrate various special days during the course of the year. These include days to meditate and pray for world transformation; Earth Day, celebrating the personhood of the earth and relationships with her; and Declaration of World Thanksgiving, an inter-faith gathering to create a 'healing force'. It is believed that, as individuals are transformed and achieve a higher sense of self-awareness by these means, so the world will ultimately be transformed. Certainly New Age practices are viewed as having a positive outcome. Paul Heelas in his book *The New Age Movement* (1996) refers to a survey of 900 adherents, of whom 82 per cent said they had become more spiritual and 80 per cent said their lives had become more meaningful. Professor John A. Saliba of the University of Detroit has suggested that there are three levels of commitment among New Agers: those who attend fairs and festivals regularly, those who consult a channeller or astrologer and those who join organized movements.

38. Satanism, the Church of Satan and the Temple of Set

Origins

There are various small, independent, Satanist groups in North America and in western Europe, but two groups have emerged with a more prominent public profile, the Church of Satan (CoS) and the Temple of Set (ToS). Satanism should not be confused with paganism, which is largely concerned with nature and fertility deities. Satanism is focused on the devil and is essentially about giving full expression to an individual's perceived needs and desires. Separate groups of Satanists understand Satan in different ways. For some in the CoS the devil is not a real being but rather a focus or icon for activities, rituals and socializing. The CoS tends to regard Satan as symbol for certain forms of violent, indulgent and vengeful behaviour and see anger, retaliation and being forceful at another's expense as types of behaviour with the potential to have a positive outcome in the life of anyone who might practise them. By contrast, the ToS understands Satan in pre-Judaic terms as 'Set', the ancient Egyptian god of death and the underworld. Set is worshipped and held by his devotees as a friend. Both the CoS and the ToS regard Satan/Set as being a role model for rebellion and self-indulgence.

In addition to these two major groups, there are others which, while not claiming to worship the devil, nevertheless make use of satanic symbolism as a means of expressing their feelings of rebellion. Such individuals may wear inverted crucifixes, watch horror films and dance to acid rock. Some Satanists do not believe in supernatural magic and assert that their ritual intentions are effected by purely psychological means. Members of both the CoS and the ToS are committed to the efficacy of supernatural magic.

The Church of Satan was founded in 1966 by Anton Szandor LaVey (formerly Howard Stanton Levy; 1930–1997). Born in Chicago on 11 April 1930, the son of Michael and Gertrude Levy, he openly declared that man's true nature is that of 'a carnal beast, living in a cosmos which is permeated and motivated by the Dark Force we call Satan'. According to his first wife, Carole, he worked for a time as the Wurlitzer organist at the Lost Weekend nightclub, supplementing his income by presenting lectures on occult topics and conducting 'witches' workshops' and eventually being advised by Edward Webber, a professional publicist of his acquaintance, that the way to increase his income would be to set up a church and get a charter from the state of California.

The CoS was founded in the summer of 1966 (not, as was later alleged, on 30 April 1966). Declaring himself to be 'the black pope', the charismatic LaVey established a structured organization, taking the title of High Priest. The church was governed by a Council of Nine, which was composed of select members of the priesthood of Mendes (Mendes being an ancient Egyptian city noted for its hedonistic festivals). The Priesthood of Mendes also acts as spokespersons for the church. Those who serve as administrators of the church are known as the Order of Trapezoid. In addition, registered members in their local areas set up a number of small self-supporting groups called 'grottos'. Their leaders are designated 'Grotto Masters'. Individuals can join the church, paying the $100 joining fee, becoming either registered members, who simply wish to declare themselves as Satanists, or active members, who play a full part in the life of a local grotto.

LaVey produced two key texts that have become influential both in CoS and beyond. These are *The Satanic Bible* (1969) and *The Satanic Rituals* (1972). Central to the church's teaching is the conviction that human beings are essentially evil with animal appetites and cravings that need to be satisfied. As one verse in the opening chapter of *The Satanic Bible* says, 'Are we not all predatory animals by instinct?' The church aims to endorse and encourage all its members to give first priority to satisfying their basic animal instincts, whether they are anger, retaliation or sexual fulfilment. Satanism on this understanding is therefore essentially both selfish and self-centred. *The Satanic Bible* is a hostile counter to basic Christian teaching: rather than reaching out to one's neighbour with love and turning the other cheek, for example, the Church of Satan's exhortation is to 'smash him on the other'.

The Temple of Set was founded in San Francisco in 1975 by Michael Aquino (b. 1946), a former US army officer from Spottswood, New Jersey, who had been a member of CoS; it can therefore be seen as a breakaway group. For LaVey the devil was in essence a symbol or role model, but for Aquino the devil was a personal being to be worshipped. ToS's aim has been described as an initiatory, magical order of the 'Left Hand Path', a term which indicates that Setians concentrate on self-refinement and self-satisfaction rather than 'Right Hand Path' goals, which are directed to an outwardly determined standard. Another statement maintains that the task of the ToS is 'not to be a saviour of the masses, but rather to encourage suitable individuals to apprehend and attain their own divinity'. For the first four years of its existence the church principally operated in San Francisco, but subsequently it spread across the USA and Canada with local grottos being established in a number of areas. Much of the church's organization is on similar lines to the CoS. Executive authority is in the hands of the Council of Nine, which appoints the High Priest and the Executive Director. Initiates are recognized in six degrees:

1. **Setian**
2. **Adept**
3. **Priest or Priestess**
4. **Magister or Magistra Templi**
5. **Magus/Maga**
6. **Ipsissimus/Ipsissima**

All the initiates in the Priesthood are highly qualified Adepts in the black arts. Fellowship is seen as important and in their first year of membership, each new Setian is required to join a local small group or 'pylon' (the name of the unique gates of the ancient Egyptian temples). Individuals who are admitted to the Temple are provided with their own copy of *The Crystal Tablet of Set*, a handbook that contains a comprehensive range of magical, philosophical and organizational information.

Core Beliefs

The entire philosophy of Satanism is laid out in *The Satanic Bible*, but LaVey also set out the nine basic beliefs:

● Satan represents indulgence instead of abstinence.
● Satan represents vital existence instead of spiritual pipe dreams.
● Satan represents undefiled wisdom instead of hypocritical self-deceit.
● Satan represents kindness to those who deserve it instead of love wasted on ingrates.
● Satan represents vengeance instead of turning the other cheek.
● Satan represents responsibility to the responsible instead of concern for psychic vampires.
● Satan represents man as just another animal – sometimes better, more often worse than those who walk on all fours – who, because of his divine spiritual and intellectual development, has become the most vicious of all.
● Satan represents all of the so-called sins, as they all lead to physical, mental, or emotional gratification.
● Satan has been the best friend the church has ever had, as he has kept it in business all these years.

Recent Developments

At the time of his death in October 1997 Anton LaVey left the Church of Satan under the command of his consort, Magistra Blanche Barton, the mother of his third son, Satan Xerxes Carnacki LaVey (b. 1993), and the church's senior administrator for the previous fifteen years. She remained at the helm as high priestess until 1997, when Peggy Nadramia succeeded her.

The CoS, reportedly, never had more than 300 members during LaVey's lifetime and the Temple of Set was estimated to have had no more than 500 members in 1990. Both the CoS and the ToS currently maintain web sites on the internet and are obviously still active. Current numbers in Britain are very small, however, and it is estimated that there are fewer than ten CoS-affiliated groups in the UK, although there may be a growing number of isolated practitioners. The 1996 Australian census gave the number of Satanists in their country as 2,091. Overall, it is doubtful whether there are more than a few thousand Satanist church worshippers in the Western world. There are a number of groups that are affiliated or influenced by LaVey's Satanism. They include a number of vampire organizations, such as the Temple of the Vampire, founded by Lucas Martel and registered in the USA in 1989.

Present Practice

LaVey used occult imagery and celebrated his own version of the Black Mass (a travesty of the Roman Catholic Mass in honour of Satan). He also distinguished three categories of satanic ritual: sex, compassion and destruction. The sex ritual could be called a love or charm spell. The compassion ritual is performed with the aim of bringing health, happiness or material status and success either to the practitioner or to another. The destruction ritual is carried out with the intention of destroying that which gets in one's way, but it is not a mandate to go out and murder someone. It is seen rather as an attempt to get rid of the extra pain and emotional pressures that are weighing a person down. In all of these rituals the individual's energy, focus and motivation are crucial. Additionally, acting out the ritual is an important factor, which aids the release of the necessary energy to bring about the intention. Rituals begin with the creation of a circle and include the use of robes, the taking of the ceremonial *athame* to call forth the demons from each compass point, and invocations to Satan to open wide the gates of hell and come forth from the abyss. It is crucially important for the individual Satanists to openly state their desire, either on paper or by symbolic actions, such as dolls dressed to represent the particular person who is the object of the ritual. Some Satanists find it helpful to record their ritual experiences in their 'grimoires'.

Members of Temple of Set also practise the full range of black arts and utilize historic Satanic imagery to assist in their rituals and to give aesthetic pleasure. In contradistinction to LaVey, the ToS maintains that humans are above the level of mere animals. They do agree that worship is essentially the worship of individualism, but it is more than merely indulging all the legal desires of the body and the ego. Setians are adamant that there are also 'higher self' aspirations. Since the Temple regards conventional religions as erroneous, it sees no point in seeking to establish relationships with them.

39. UFO religions, the Aetherius Society, the Raëlian Church, Heaven's Gate

39a. UFO religions

Origins

From the seventeenth century onwards people claimed to have seen celestial objects and have maintained that they had been transported to other planets. However, the beginning of the modern UFO movement has been dated from 24 June 1947, when Kenneth Arnold was piloting a small aircraft and reportedly saw nine shiny, metallic objects that 'flew like a saucer would if you skipped it across water'.

By the close of 1947 there had been over 850 reported UFO sightings, although none was seen by a large group of people. The most celebrated instance was a 1947 sighting at Roswell, New Mexico, where there was a large explosion and chunks of fractured metal were left scattered over a wide area. Initially the US Air Force passed it off as the crash of a piece of dysfunctional weather apparatus, but an investigation in 1980 led some to conclude that it was a UFO. Since that time Roswell has become a sacred place for ufologists.

These incidents gave rise to the use of the term 'flying saucer' and sparked a growing interest in the UFO phenomenon. Further waves of interest were sparked off by films such as *The Day the Earth Stood Still* (1951), *Close Encounters of The Third Kind* (1977) and *ET, the Extraterrestrial* (1982) as well as by the publication of books such as Erich von Däniken's *Chariots of the Gods* (1969). Coupled with this, a growing number of individuals began to adopt ETs as spiritual guides, believing them to be scientifically and technologically superior to other categories of spirit guides. The element of mystery surrounding UFOs led to their being accorded divine status and inevitably some adherents began to link the UFOs with the celestial chariots of Old Testament prophets, Ezekiel and Elijah. UFO religions have been defined as having a focus on flying saucers and a belief that they contain extraterrestrials who have travelled to earth to warn of impending disasters and to offer help and protection. The primary assertion of UFO groups is that there is intelligent life outside of planet earth. Within each UFO group there appear to be a select few who are able to make contact with these extraterrestrials or 'star brothers'; they are designated 'contactees' and in consequence become their movements' leaders; the membership put their faith in the reports and leadership of these men and women and this binds them into a tightly knit community. UFO devotees believe that each individual evolves from one life to the next, so that every entity within the universe is interrelated.

Earlier movements such as the Theosophical Society believed in 'Ascended Masters' whose teachings were 'channelled' to particular individuals such as Helena Blavatsky (*see* The Theosophical Movement) or Alice Bailey (*see* New Age Religion). In ufology one essential difference is that these god-like beings visit earth in the form of extraterrestrials and communicate by direct encounters. Ufology makes use of major religious doctrines such as God, karma and reincarnation, but it has, as Professor Christopher Partridge of University College Chester has pointed out, an essentially 'physicalist' aspect. This is seen in the importance attached to flying saucers, astronauts, extraterrestrials and abduction incidents. This has endeared ufism to those sections of society who have a more secular and scientific world-view. Some groups such as the Raëlians lay much more emphasis on the physical/scientific phenomena than others.

Many thousands of people claim to have encountered or been abducted by aliens. A good proportion of abductees appear to be positive about these encounters and claim their experience to have been a spiritual and divine encounter. Others are altogether more anxious and believe that some of these visitors from outer space are evil and malignant beings that rape, torture and murder. Some writers, such as the former Coventry City footballer and TV commentator David Icke (b. 1952), are convinced that many of the world's leaders are masquerading Reptilians. By this he means that extraterrestrials (Reptilians) have either possessed these leaders or are manipulating them.

Core Beliefs

UFO groups share a number of common beliefs.
● There is no spiritual creator, only aliens with superior science seeding planets.

- There are intelligent beings outside this planet and some individuals are capable of contact with them.
- All supernatural phenomena can be explained in terms of physical alien visitations.

Recent Developments

In recent times a number of UFO religious and quasi-religious institutions have been established. Prominent among them are the Atherius Society founded in England by Dr George King in 1955, the Raëlian Church formed in France by Claude Vorilhon in 1973 and Heaven's Gate, which was established by Marshall Herff Applewhite and Bonnie Lu Trusdale Nettles in the USA in 1975.

39b. The Aetherius Society

Origins

The Aetherius Society was established by Dr George King (1919–97). Born in Shropshire, England, King was brought up in a traditional Christian environment, but developed an interest in psychic phenomena and yoga, which he studied for ten years. During this period he often practised yogic exercises for up to twelve hours a day. On 8 May 1954, while alone in his London apartment, he heard a loud voice that commanded him: 'Prepare yourself! You are to become the voice of Interplanetary Parliament.'

The message was given by an Ascended Master called Aetherius, who came from the planet Venus. Aetherians believe that King was chosen to receive this message because he was a master of yoga (raja, gnani and kundalini) known as Samadhi. Shortly after his encounter, King was visited by a world-renowned yoga master and given a set of exercises to enable him to establish mental contact with the 'Cosmic Masters' who inhabit the higher planes of other planets. According to the Society's official web site, it was for this reason that the Cosmic Masters of the Solar System began to use him as 'Primary Terrestrial Mental Channel' to transmit their messages to earth.

Guided by cosmic powers, King settled in the USA in 1959 and the following year the Aetherius Society was incorporated as a non-profit organization. During the next twenty years King continued to act as Primary Terrestrial Mental Channel and recorded over 600 cosmic transmissions. During his life King also accomplished a number of cosmic missions, which are believed to have resulted in global healing and an improved karmic balance for the human race. Between 1958 and 1961, for example, he completed a major mission called Operation Starlight. He climbed to the top of nearly twenty holy mountains, where he facilitated the transmission of a charge of spiritual energy from the Cosmic Masses. This energy is now stored in these mountains so that others can make pilgrimages there and pray for healing.

Aetherians maintain that many of the flying saucers that are sighted are simply ensuring the protection of their activities and the well-being of Mother Earth. King, who in 1981 was crowned Metropolitan Archbishop of Aetherius Churches and Prince Grand Master of the Mystical Order of St Peter, died on 12 July 1997 in Santa Barbara, California. Central to Aetherian belief is the law of karma that has been taught in the East throughout history. Aetherians find echoes of it both in the New Testament principle that 'a man reaps what he sows' (Galatians 6:7) and in the words of the Buddha, who declared 'action and reaction are opposite and equal'.

Core Beliefs

● All things are living, including Mother Earth.
● The law of karma; 'As you sow, so shall you reap.'
● The law of reincarnation (life being a journey back to One Creative Source, our progress being determined by the way in which we live each separate life).
● Contact with extraterrestrial Cosmic Masters and Ascended Masters brings benefit to humankind.

Recent Developments

The Aetherius Society has its US headquarters in Los Angeles and main European base in London. There are three levels of membership (Friend, Full and Associate), progressively requiring increased levels of commitment and subscription. Full members are expected to observe spiritual commemorations throughout the year, including 8 July, which marks the Cosmic Initiation of the earth. The commemoration services are held at Aetherian centres around the world. The current number of adherents is probably somewhere around 15,000 to 20,000. The movement is reported as having around 10,000 on its UK mailing list alone. It produces its own journal, *Cosmic Voice*.

Present Practice

King had an intense personal encounter with the Ascended Master Jesus on top of Holdstone Down in Devon on 23 July 1958. Following this, on twelve consecutive Sundays, he received the Twelve Blessings, which are an extension of the Sermon on the Mount with practical and mystical rituals. Each branch of the Aetherian Society holds regular weekly services in a temple on Sundays at 11 a.m. and on Thursdays in the evening. These consist of prayer and readings that are taken from the Aquarian Age Bible and the Twelve Blessings.

39c. The Raëlian Church

Origins

The Raëlian movement hit the world headlines at the end of 2002, when they claimed to have cloned the world's first baby. Their founder was Claude Vorilhon (b. 1946), who was born and raised in France, where he worked as a motor-racing journalist and a singer. In 1973, whilst visiting a volcanic region near Clermont-Ferrand, he encountered a small spacecraft, out of which a bearded man appeared, barely over a metre tall. The man began to engage him in conversation. He claimed to be one of the Elohim and said, 'We are the ones who made all life on earth, you mistook us for gods, we were at the origin of your main religions, now that you are mature enough to understand this, we would like to enter official contact through an embassy.'

The extraterrestrial explained to Vorilhon that, although *elohim* is often translated as 'God' in the Old Testament, the word is a plural form and means 'those who come from the sky'. It was these beings who had created the human race by the manipulation of DNA.

Those with enough Hebrew had always known that *elohim*, which occurs some 2,570 times in the Old Testament, was the plural of *eloah*; and the German scholar Franz Delitzsch (1813–90), professor of Theology at Leipzig and expert in Hebrew, had long taught that, when used to refer to the God of the Jews, *elohim* may be regarded as a 'plural of intensity', emphasizing that Yhwh is the totality of all that is divine (in contrast to the multiplicity of individual gods in polytheism) or a 'plural of majesty'. The astonishing part of the little man's news was not his grammar point, but his revelation that a race of extraterrestrial scientists was responsible for the creation of the world and humankind.

The Raëlians draw attention to passages in the Old Testament such as Genesis 6:1–4, which are interpreted to mean that extraterrestrials visited earth, engaged in sexual relationships with the women of Israel and thereby produced a race of giants or people of great intelligence.

Vorilhon was given the name Raël (said to mean 'the light of the Elohim') and in 1975 he was taken to the planet Elohim in a flying saucer and introduced to a number of famous prophets, including the Buddha, Confucius, Jesus and Joseph Smith (*see* The Church of Jesus Christ of the Latter-Day Saints). The Elohim, described as small humanoids with light green skin and elongated eyes, asked Raël to prepare an embassy in Jerusalem for them to return to in 2035. The embassy was not only to receive extraterrestrial visitors, but also to host an annual gathering of

144,000 Raëlians. Raël (formerly Vorilhon) has given details of his encounters with extraterrestrials in two publications: *The Book Which Tells the Truth* (1974) and *Extraterrestrials Took Me to Their Planet* (1975).

Core Beliefs

● The Elohim are the creators of humanity.
● An embassy must be built to receive the Elohim.
● The world has entered the last age, the 'Age of Apocalypse', in which humanity has the capacity to destroy itself totally.
● DNA is the source of eternal life.
● There will be a one world government, ruled by a 'geniocracy' (those who are 50 per cent more intelligent than average).
● Raël is the new messiah. His role is to inaugurate the new society when the Elohim arrive on earth. Crime will be solved by genetic engineering.

Recent Developments

In order to fund the construction of the new embassy, members must donate 10 per cent of their annual salary. However, despite modifying their swastika symbol, the Raëlians have so far failed to gain the confidence of the Israeli authorities. In the meantime Raël is continuing with his commission to spread peace and sensual meditation to humankind. Raëlians reject what they regard as the repressive elements of Christianity. They welcome extramarital sex, homosexuality and nudity.

The Raëlians run a number of projects, including Clonaid, founded in 1997 and headed by a Raëlian bishop, Dr Brigitte Boisselier (b. 1956), to enable subscribers to have their own cloned replica by depositing a sample of their DNA while they are alive. After the terrorist attacks on the World Trade Towers and the Pentagon on 11 September 2001, Raëlians proposed the use of cloning to restore crime victims to life and to recreate suicide bombers so that they might receive suitable punishment.

Since 1973 Raëlianism has expanded to a 2002 membership of 55,000 in 84 countries, although Raël says only about 10 per cent are active. The religion is strongest in French-speaking Canada, French-speaking Europe and Japan. There are currently about 1,000 active Raëlians in the UK.

Present Practice

Raëlians stress the importance of sensual meditation, which is designed to exercise and develop the senses. At some meetings sexual techniques are taught, including how to caress breasts and nipples; individuals are encouraged to experiment sexually if they wish and to develop their sensuality. This aspect of Raëlianism has met with criticism on the part of those who seek to uphold traditional family values. New members are recruited into the movement from the internet and by invitations to Sensual Seminars. There have been some reports of Raëlian women attracting recruits by offering free sex.

39d. Heaven's Gate

Origins

Heaven's Gate church was founded by Marshall Herff Applewhite (1931–97), the son of a Presbyterian music director and later university professor of music, and Bonnie Lu Trusdale Nettles (1955–85), a former Baptist and registered nurse, following an experience that convinced them they were the two witnesses mentioned in the New Testament, Revelation 11. In 1973 Nettles left her husband and four children to go with Applewhite. The fundamental belief of Heaven's Gate was that because humans are souls using bodies as a vehicle to progress to a 'level above human', they would need to shed their earthly containers. Heaven's Gate initially believed that the chosen would ascend bodily to a UFO, but, following the death from cancer of Nettles, who clearly did not ascend bodily, they taught that the body would be left behind.

The two founders took the symbolic names 'Bo' and 'Peep' to mark their role as shepherds who aimed to lead their flock aboard UFOs up to a level above human. Heaven's Gate effectively began in 1975 at Waldport, Oregon, when Bo and Peep, who were on a recruitment tour, met Clarence Klug, a New Age teacher. He had brought together a small group of about twenty and was teaching them that they could reach God by means of a special exercise routine. This involved opening up seven divine energy centres situated along the spine, enabling the body to become 'divine light, transcending all physical limitations and karmic laws'. Klug's following had become somewhat disillusioned with his teachings, but were attracted by Applewhite and Nettles' more literal assertion that spaceships would carry individuals up to the next level. Klug's group had followed a fairly libertine agenda, practising regular sexual relations in order to create the energy that would enable them to become divine light. Bo and Peep's ideas on the matter were radically different. They established a sex-free environment, where women did not wear clothing which emphasized their femininity and some men were castrated. Members had their hair cropped short and wore black baggy clothes to make them appear genderless. Sex, alcohol and tobacco were taboo. According to Michael Conyers, a member from 1975 to 1988, he was 'mesmerized' by Applewhite's teaching, an unusual synthesis of occult spirituality and UFO soteriology.

Core Beliefs

- The world is under assault by evil aliens who keep human beings bound to continuous reincarnations on earth.
- Applewhite and Nettles (Bo and Peep) are the two prophets described in Revelation 11:11–13. They will lead a small chosen group of people to a level above human.
- Heaven's Gate members will ascend bodily to flying saucers.
- The chosen group will subsequently become crew members on UFOs.
- Heaven is literal and physical and will be enjoyed by the raptured members of HG.

Recent Developments

The group disappeared from public view for almost twenty years and for the most part they lived in communes. After nearly twenty-two years they took up residence in Rancho Santa Fe, a few miles north of San Diego, where they ran an IT business called Higher Source, which designed web sites. The environment of Heaven's Gate was highly structured and particularly strict. Their regime was reported to be increasingly dominated and controlled by the dictates of Applewhite. Former member Conyers stated that even the pancakes had to be cooked in a particular way. They also began to isolate themselves from their families and the outside world.

Present Practice

The group finally achieved notoriety on 27 March 1997, when all 39 members committed mass suicide, their action apparently triggered by the appearance of the comet Hale-Bopp. This was taken to be the UFO with extraterrestrials aboard that had come to take them on to a level above human.

40. Paganism, Wicca, Druidry, the Northern Tradition, Shamanism and Heathenism

Paganism is a vital living religion that is both old and new. It has its roots in the ancient nature religions of Europe, but in more recent times, particularly since the 1960s, it has been filling a felt spiritual need on the part of many people in the Western world. Paganism is an umbrella term that embraces Wicca (also called witchcraft), Druidry, Shamanism and the Northern Tradition or *Ásatrú* (meaning 'true to the Aesir', the Norse gods). In 1971 the Pagan Federation was established as an umbrella organization to provide contact between these different groups, all of which reverence and respect the earth and its peoples. This high regard for nature leads not only to the valuing and practice of natural medicine, but also to a recognition of spirits of place and of the earth itself, which is believed by many to be a single living organism, the goddess Gaia. Modern paganism celebrates nature as well as many gods and goddesses. Those whose commitment is towards the Great Mother Earth often call themselves Ecopagans. Others represent themselves in terms of the particular tradition that they follow, which may be Wiccan, witch, Druid, Odinist, shaman or goddess-worshipper.

Modern pagans recognize the divine as transcending gender and acknowledging both male and female. They also stress the importance of a love for, and kinship with, nature and emphasize a positive morality that is encapsulated by the sentence, 'Do what you will, as long as it harms none.'

The massive American Religion Identification Survey (ARIS) taken in 2001 estimated there were 140,000 pagans in the USA.

40a. Wicca

Origins

The word 'witch' comes from the Anglo-Saxon 'wicce', which indicated pagan and magical practice. Witchcraft is also called 'Wicca' or 'the Craft'. All witches are pagans, but not all pagans are witches. Wiccans meet regularly for social and religious purposes in small groups of like-minded people called 'covens'. At some of these meetings they may practise either natural or high magic. The former involves utilizing earth's resources, such as herbs or crystals, to effect change, including healing the sick. 'High magic' (often spelled 'magick') involves rituals and it aims to make contact with the divine. Some witches do not to belong to a coven and work on their own. They are designated 'hedge witches'.

Wiccans should not be confused with Satanists. They do not worship the devil or demons. Throughout history many witches suffered very harsh punishments on account of this misunderstanding. Much of the extreme cruelty that was meted out followed the publication of *Malleus Maleficarum* (1486). This book, which was compiled by two monks, became the mandate for the Inquisition. It speaks about the depravity of witches, outlines their activities and lays down the procedure for witch trials. For example, the book states that, first the jailers prepare the implements of torture, then they strip the prisoner; then the judge 'tries to persuade the prisoner to confess the truth freely'. If no confession is forthcoming, 'he bids the attendants make the prisoner fast to the Strappado or some other implement of torture.' One of the last witch-hunts in the West took place in the town of Salem, Massachusetts, in 1692. Twenty people were executed. As to the origins of witchcraft, some scholars are of the view that its origins lie in the ancient pre-Christian traditions of the Middle East.

Core Beliefs

- The pentagram has been firmly established as a Wiccan symbol since the late 1960s. The five spiked wards are taken to represent five elements in order of density; earth, water, air, fire and spirit (aether). These in turn stand for other qualities; earth for wisecraft, water for love and worship, air for knowledge, fire for magic and spirit for mysticism. Wiccans' five basic beliefs are:

  1. 'If it harm none, do what you will.'
  2. The law of attraction
  3. Harmony and serenity
  4. Power through knowledge
  5. Progressive reincarnation.

- God is immanent and transcendent.
- Divinity manifests itself through all living beings.

- Every living entity has a spirit that is connected to and part of every other spirit.
- God and goddess images are recognized as aspects of a greater divinity.

Recent Developments

Since the middle of the twentieth century there has been a rapid resurgence of Wicca. A major factor in this was the repeal in 1951 of the Witchcraft Act of 1735, which had ruled that witchcraft was a criminal offence. This meant that Britain's witches, who reportedly numbered 45,000, no longer needed to keep a low profile and that books and journals relating to the Craft could be freely printed and circulated. Among those whose writings were influential in this burgeoning of paganism were the scholar Margaret Murray (1863–1963) – whose *The Witch-Cult in Western Europe* (1921) contended that witchcraft was well established before the birth of Christianity, but was then suppressed by the church – and, more particularly, Gerald Gardner (1884–1964) and Doreen Valiente (1922–99). Murray's work is painstakingly detailed and contains information on such issues as how the devil was perceived in medieval covens, how dancing was conducted and how the god of the witches is a lineal descendant of a palaeolithic goat or stag god who later became the Celtic horned god Cernunnos.

Gerald Gardner, a one-time curator of the Isle of Man's witchcraft museum, published *Witchcraft Today* in 1954. It was the first-ever non-fiction book on Wicca. Indeed Gardner is regarded by some as the first person ever to practise Wicca in a recognisably modern form. His teaching focused on the Mother

Goddess and his strongly held belief in reincarnation. In 1953 Gardner initiated Doreen Valiente into the Craft, using his own *Book of Shadows*. Valiente, who had a Christian upbringing, had begun to practise witchcraft in her teenage years and is hailed by many practising pagans as 'the mother of modern witchcraft'. Her contribution to the development of Wiccan ritual cannot be overstated. However, she left Gardner's coven in 1957 describing him as 'a thoroughly kinky old goat who was into flagellation' and began working with the hereditary witch, Robert Cochrane (1931–66). After the death of her husband in 1972, she turned her attention to writing and her books *The ABC of Witchcraft* (1973) and *Natural Magic* (1975) established her as a worldwide authority on magic and Wicca. The latter volume contains a great deal of basic information, right down to detailed herbal remedies and the kind of stones to wear to bring peace.

The American Religion Identification Survey of 2001 estimated there were 134,000 Wiccans in the USA. In the 2001 UK decennial census 40,000 people reported their religion as either Pagan or Wiccan.

Present Practice

Wiccans observe eight festivals, called Sabbats, and as with all pagan rites these are linked to the seasons of the year that are seen as a wheel. As the wheel revolves, so nature reveals the faces of the gods. These celebrations reflect the male and female aspect of nature. This is often achieved by means of sacred dance by the men and women of the coven, naked to indicate being at one with nature. The equal division of the sexes in the modern coven was one of Dr Gardner's contributions to the Craft; in medieval times men were in the majority. The worship site is newly constructed for each occasion. A consecrated circle marks them out and only coven members may enter the inmost circle. In an initiation of witches, novices are naked and blindfolded to test their trust in witchcraft. Other ceremonies include 'Wiccaning', which is an equivalent of baptism. The ceremony takes place in a circle with a cauldron in the centre and altar to one side, close to which are gifts for the child. Invocations are made to the great god, Cernunnos. The high priest in the case of a boy, or high priestess in the case of a girl, asks 'the blessing of the mighty God and the gentle Goddess' on the child. The mother brings the child forward to be blessed and it is then that child's Craft name is revealed, which can later be adopted if he or she chooses the Wiccan path. The child is then anointed on the forehead with the pentagram. The eight annual festivals that take place in the open air are as follows.

1. Samhaim or All Hallows Eve on 31 October is the festival of the dead, in which all pagans remember those who have gone before.
2. Midwinter or Yule on 21 December is the winter solstice, when the sun child is reborn. It is regarded as the New Year.
3. Imbolc (also Oimelc or Candlemas) on or around 1 February celebrates the awakening of the sun and heralds the spring.
4. The spring equinox on 21 March celebrates fertility and many pagans dedicate this time to Eostre, the Anglo-Saxon goddess of fertility.
5. Beltane on 30 April is celebrated with maypole dances that symbolize the mystery of the sacred marriage of goddess and god.

6. Midsummer or summer solstice on 21 June, sometimes called Litha, is a celebration of light.

7. Lughnasadh or Lammas is the time of corn harvest, when pagans give thanks for the provision of the goddess as Queen of the Land.

8. The autumn equinox is kept on 21 September and for many pagans this is a time to honour old age and the approach of winter.

40b. Druidry

Origins

The word 'Druid' may be derived from the Celtic prefix *dru-* meaning 'wise one'. Druids tend to focus on the sun, whereas Wiccans are centred on the moon. As with Wicca, Druidry is diverse in its thinking and practice. Its origins lie in Celtic traditions, gods and goddesses. Druids also have a great love for the poetic, healing, divination and sacred mythology. Not all Druids are pagans, some are simply artistic and cultural, and some have Christian convictions. Many present-day Druids maintain that the most long-standing order of Druidry which holds ceremonies at Stonehenge is the Ancient Druid Order founded in London in 1717 by John Toland. Others take the view that the earliest revived Druid order was the Ancient Order of Druids founded in 1781 by Henry Hurle. The United Ancient Order of Druids developed out of these earlier groups in 1833.

Core Beliefs

● There are many gods and goddesses.
● Nature is the embodiment of the gods.
● All life is sacred and should not be taken without
   deliberation or regard.
● The spirit is immortal.
● Morality is personal and based on respect for others.

Recent Developments

The origins of Druidry in recent times includes the British Druid
Order, founded in 1979, which is both pagan and goddess-
orientated and the Order of Bards, Ovates and Druids (OBOD),
founded in 1964 by Ross Nichols, which has both Christian and
pagan members. The Bards are keepers of the tradition, the
Ovates are trained in prophecy and the Druids are regarded as
counsellors. The London Druid group that was established in
1986 has links with both Celtic and magic groups. The Secular
Order of Druids that dates from the same year is strongly
focused on environmental and civil rights issues. The Gorsedd of
Bards of Caer Abiri, which was founded in 1993, has a multi-faith
foundation and celebrates the major Druid festivals at the
Avebury stone circle in Wiltshire, England. In the UK 2001
census the number giving their religion as Druidism was 1,657.

Present Practice

Druids are polytheists who believe that a deity that is both male
and female exists in all things. They are effectually animists,

maintaining that the deity exists in all living things, human, animal and divine. Druids live in close touch with nature and whenever possible hold their ritual celebrations in the open air. Druids are more organized than Wicca and local Druid groups (or 'groves') belong to a particular Druid Order.

40c. The Northern Tradition, Shamanism and Heathenism

Origins

Some pagans draw their spirituality and belief systems from what has become known as the Northern Tradition, rather than from the Middle Eastern and central European traditions. For this reason some of their number favour the term 'heathen' as opposed to pagan.

The Northern Tradition draws largely from the Norse and Icelandic pre-Christian mythologies and traditions. This embraces the sky gods (*Aesir*) of the Scandinavian myths, including the High God (or All-father principle) Odin and his wife Frigga, together with Thor, Tyr and Balder. Also part of this tradition are the *Vanir* or fertility gods of the earth and agriculture. The Northern Tradition has become increasingly popular with those who want to cultivate in their own lives the qualities of loyalty, honour and courage. Followers of Odin are very taken up with environmental issues and attach high importance to celebrating the seasonal festivals.

Shamanism is part of many Wiccan and Druidic movements. The word *shaman* comes from a Siberian dialect word (*samen*) and denotes 'an ascetic' or 'one who works alone'. The Siberian shamans healed the sick and led the souls of the departed to the world of the dead. Shamanism is perhaps the oldest known form of spirituality in the world. Essentially it is the practice of trance and bodiless travel, together with the ability to overcome evil powers by casting spells through intense feats of concentration. By these means the practitioner is able to prognosticate the future and convey healing and wholeness.

Core Beliefs

There are no fixed sets of belief. Each shaman, who may be either a man or a woman, follows his or her own pathway. Many shamans are also diviners in respect of both the past and the future.

Recent Developments

In the contemporary context Shamans are frequently sought after by those who have lost faith in traditional religious practice and are searching for a higher level of spiritual awareness. Despite its ancient origins, Shamanism is enjoying increasing popularity among the peoples of the developed nations. Shamanism is closely linked to what has been termed techno-Shamanism, which utilizes rave music and hallucinogenic drugs. Some practitioners of Shamanism have developed this practice of techno-Shamanism, but the core of Shamanism remains distinct from this strand. Shamanism is a growing new religion in a number of countries in western Europe and most notably in the USA, where the American anthropologist Michael Haner has been influential. His Foundation for Shamanic Studies at Mill Valley, California, offers training courses in core Shamanism, which attract more than 5,000 people each year. Shamanism remains widespread within communities around the world that uphold indigenous religions. It is estimated that the overall number of those who engage in Shamanistic practice is over 12 million. In South Korea 5 per cent of the population claim Shamanism as their religion.

Present Practice

The goal of Shamanism is to reach a point where the soul is believed to have left the body and is therefore free to travel and reach another dimension and level of spiritual experience. This separation of the soul from the body is achieved in a variety of ways. These include rhythmic drumming, ecstatic dance and the use of certain kinds of plants. Once in an out-of-body experience, the shaman is able to receive healing power or guidance for the future.

Along with Wicca, most Druids and those of the Northern Tradition celebrate the wheel and also have a deep concern regarding the ecological crisis.

Glossary

acupuncture An ancient Chinese medicinal practice in which needles are inserted into the skin at specific points as a way of improving health.

adept A person believed, by theosophists and some New Age groups, to be skilled in supernatural knowledge and powers.

adventism The belief that Christ will come to reign on earth at the end of human history.

Agonshu A Japanese new religion with around 300,000 followers, founded in 1978 and drawing on Buddhism. It teaches that freedom from bad karma can be achieved through good deeds and meditation.

antitypical Predicted or foreshadowed (for example, by an event or prophecy in the Old Testament); a method of biblical interpretation used by David Koresh, in which he saw himself as foreshadowed by several biblical characters, such as Cyrus, Elijah and David.

Armageddon A mountain (Hebrew: *har*) overlooking the plain of Megiddo, in the biblical tradition the place where the last battle takes place before the final judgment.

ashram In Indian religion a place of retreat; a hermitage, a monastery or simply a communal house for devotees of a guru.

athame An altar tool used in Satanic rituals, traditionally a double-bladed knife with a black handle.

atman The Sanskrit word for one's soul, inner self or true self (in Pali the term is *atta*): a vital element in Hinduism and religions derived from it, including Buddhism and ISKCON.

avatar ('One who descends'); usually an incarnation on earth of the Hindu god Vishnu, his most famous avatar taking the form of Krishna, although some modern cults claim to worship a living avatar.

Baba A Hindu title similar in meaning to 'Saint'.

babu A traditional Hindu title of respect (for a Hindu gentleman).

Balder The fairest of the Norse gods, god of light, joy, purity, beauty, innocence and reconciliation; son of Odin and Frigga.

baptism in the spirit An overwhelming experience of love and the presence of God that is brought about by the Holy Spirit as on the Day of Pentecost (see Acts 2:1–11); often accompanied by speaking in tongues.

Bhagavad Gita A major Hindu sacred text (literally 'song of the Lord'), a dialogue section of the epic Mahabarata in which the avatar Krishna speaks to a prince about wisdom and actions and consequences.

Bhagavan/Bhagwan An Indian title meaning 'Lord' or 'worshipful'; a title of honour used of holy men by devotees; a title for God or a man claiming to be God.

bhikku/bhikkhu A Buddhist (mendicant) monk.

bodhisattva In Mahayana Buddhism a spiritually superior or heavenly being who is in a state of bliss but continues to help human beings still seeking enlightenment.

Brahma The creator god of Hinduism, together with Vishnu and Shiva one part of a triadic way of understanding God.

Brahman In Hinduism the ultimate, absolute, non-personal, divine reality of the universe, from which all being originates and to which all being returns.

caste The Hindu custom and belief that every Indian, as a consequence of his or her actions in a previous life, is born into a specific social class that has particular occupations and concepts of purity and pollution attached to it.

Cernunnos The Celtic horned god of fertility, usually depicted with the antlers of a stag.

chakra In yoga any of the seven main points on the body through which spiritual energy passes.

charismatic In Christianity (the quality of) one who emphasizes the power and presence of the Holy Spirit and emphasizes and practises the biblical gifts of the Holy Spirit, such as prophecy, healing and speaking in tongues; in general use, (the quality of) someone of inspiring leadership who stimulates enthusiasm and devotion.

chela In Indian religion a novice or follower of a guru; in the Church Universal and Triumphant (CUT) or in Eckankar a disciple of a spiritual master.

creedal Christianity Any form of Christianity based on the doctrines of the three great historic Christian creeds: the Apostles' Creed, the Nicene Creed and the Athanasian Creed.

Dada In Indian religion an affectionate term of respect for a saintly man, as with the founder of the Brahma Kumaris, known as Dada Lekhraj: 'venerable (old) Lekhraj'.

Dadi In Indian religion an affectionate term of respect for a saintly woman (*see* Dada).

Deva A god or demi-god of the Hindu pantheon.

dhamma A Pali word for dharma, as used in an ancient Theravada Buddhist canon.

dharma A Sanskrit word that in Hinduism means cosmic law, the law of existence, right conduct; also, in Buddhism, the teaching of the Buddha, religious truth.

dispensationalism A scheme taught by fundamentalist Christians in the USA which divides history into seven dispensations or periods of time.

eck In Eckankar the life force or holy spirit.

ectoplasm A glutinous substance that may come out of a medium who is in a trance state.

engram A harmful or painful memory that Scientologists hope to treat.

esoteric (Of hidden, inner spiritual knowledge) that is accessible only to the initiated.

Falun Gong A series of exercises designed to produce spiritual energy.

Frigga The wife of Odin, the Scandinavian high god.

fundamentalists Those who regard the Bible or some other sacred text as their supreme authority and interpret it with great literalness.

Gaia The mother goddess, Earth.

gnani Light, knowledge.

Gnosticism A system of secret, experiential or mystical knowledge, which asserts that matter is evil and that salvation involves the freeing of the divine spark that is trapped in the human body.

gong   The cultivation of energy.

grimoire   A book of Black Magic giving information on raising spirits.

guru   A spiritual teacher, especially one offering teaching in Hinduism or a Hindu-derived religion.

Hadith   The traditions of the Prophet Muhammad's words and deeds (Shi'ite Muslims denying the reliability of the Sunni Muslim version and accepting only those that come directly from the Prophet's family.)

Hare   In Hinduism 'the spirit of God'.

Hazrat   A Muslim saint.

japa   Meditation using the repetition of the name of God, as in ISKCON.

Kabbalah   An esoteric system of mystical knowledge derived from ancient Jewish sources; also any occult lore that is used in magic.

kalyana   Spiritual friendship, as promoted by the Western Buddhist Order (from Sanskrit: 'celebration').

karma   A person's actions, which may be either good or bad, and by implication the consequences of those actions.

kirtan   Chanting songs of praise, as in ISKCON.

Krishna   In Hindu tradition the eighth avatar or incarnation of the god Vishnu, appearing as the divine hero of the epic Mahabarata, including the section called the Bhagavad Gita.

kundalini   In yoga a form of spiritual energy that passes through the body, often held to reside at the base of the spine.

Laksmi   A major Hindu goddess, who represents wealth and prosperity.

lama   A Tibetan Buddhist monk.

Lotus Sutra   A key text in Mahayana Buddhism, teaching that anyone can attain enlightenment.

Mahayana   A devotional school of Buddhism that developed between 100 BCE and CE 100, some forms of which emphasize direct teaching from teacher to pupil rather than from a written text.

mala   In Hinduism a string of beads or knots used in meditation and prayer; for Hare Krishna devotees a string of 108 beads used for chanting.

mantra A verbal sound which devotees either chant out aloud or repeat mentally to enable them to tune into God.

medium A person, in spiritualism in particular, who receives messages from the past for devotees.

millenarianism The belief that at the end of the present age there will be a long period – in some religions a literal thousand years (millennium) – of bliss on this earth.

monism The belief that there is one basis or principle that underlies the whole universe.

Narayana A name for Vishnu, one of the three supreme gods of Hinduism.

occult Hidden wisdom or spiritual forces.

Odin The Scandinavian high god, husband of Frigga.

paganism An umbrella term that embraces Wicca (witchcraft), Druidry, Ásatrú and Shamanism.

Parsi A descendant of the ancient Zoroastrian Persians, living largely in India and practising an ethical monotheism with a marked ritual life focusing on purity.

puja In Hinduism or Hindu-derived religions an act of worship or reverence in a temple; a ceremony of a similar nature.

Radha The mistress of Krishna in the Mahabharata, their relationship being seen by some Hindus as representing the love between God and the soul, the eroticism of the narrative not welcomed by all.

raja A form of yoga that seeks to bring the mind and emotions into balance so that the attention can be easily focused on the object of meditation.

Rama In Hindu tradition the seventh avatar of the god Vishnu, whose exploits in love and war are described in the Ramayana (one of the two great epics of the Hindu scriptures, compiled in the second or first century BCE); the epitome of righteousness and moral virtue.

reincarnation The rebirth of the soul in a different bodily form (in successive lives).

restorationism A movement seeking to restore the apostolic New Testament form of Christianity to the contemporary church.

samadhi In Hinduism and Buddhism a state of deep meditation leading to a higher spiritual state, which may be achieved through yoga.

sankirtana In Hinduism a form of religious singing or chanting praises to God.

sannyasi/sannyasin In Sanskrit 'one who abandons'; a Hindu ascetic who has attained the last of the four Stages of Life and seeks liberation as a wandering beggar.

satsang A religious gathering; in Sikhism a congregation (of men and women).

Set/Seth The ancient Egyptian god of storms and the underworld; violent and dangerous, he murdered his brother Osiris, the god of fertility and symbol of death and resurrection.

Shakti/Sakti In Hinduism or Hindu-derived religions the female principle or organ of reproduction and generative power; also this principle as manifested by, for example, Kali, consort of the god Shiva.

Shamanism Religious practice based on a belief that the world is full of good and evil spirits that can be influenced by a shaman, an initiate with the ability to go into a trance state through dance or ecstasy.

Shiva/Siva One of the two great gods of Hindu devotion (see Vishnu); a god of contrasts, he presides over creation and destruction, fertility and asceticism, good and evil, personal destinies; his name means 'auspicious'.

Shree/Shri Variant spellings of Sri.

soteriology Teaching about salvation.

Sri/Shri/Shree In the Indian subcontinent, or in a Hindu-derived religion, a respectful title preceding the name of a god, a sacred text or a distinguished person; in some contexts similar to 'Mr'.

Sufism A mystical and devotional form of Islam.

Sugmad In Eckankar a sacred name for God, neither masculine nor feminine, the source of all life.

sutra In Buddhism, a discourse by the Buddha or a teaching by an authorized follower.

symbology In religion, the practice of learning to receive the divine presence through clearing the mind and meditating on symbols.

t'ai chi A form of exercise for maintaining health and wholeness, of which certain forms can also be used for self-defence.

Tantrism A range of Indian and Tibetan spiritual practices which, in some forms, includes the use of sex and the physical senses to increase divine consciousness.

tarot A deck of seventy-eight cards (four suits of 14 cards, the minor arcana, and 22 other cards, the major arcana) used for fortune-telling.

theogamy The marriage between God and a human being.

thetan The term given by Scientologists to designate a person's spiritual nature.

Thor The Norse god of thunder, usually depicted with a hammer, the defender of humans against giants.

trinitarian The Christian belief that God is revealed and known as Father, Son and Holy Spirit.

Tyr The oldest of the Norse gods, god of war and of justice; the counterpart of the Anglo-Saxon god Tiu.

UFO Unidentified flying object or 'flying saucer'.

universalism A doctrine that all will ultimately be saved; modified universalism, by contrast, holds that all will have a further opportunity after death to accept or reject the offer of salvation.

Vanir A group of nature gods and goddesses considered to bring health, youth, fertility and wealth.

Vedas Sacred scriptures expressing the religion of the Aryan people of India, comprising Rig Veda (hymns to the gods), Sama Veda (verses for chanting), Yajur Veda (prose instructions relating to ritual) and Atharva Veda (rites and spells in verse, especially concerned with curing illness).

Vishnu One of the three great gods of Hinduism (*see* Brahma, Shiva), preserver and life-giver, creator of the cosmos, whose appearance on earth from time to time as an avatar is intended to reawaken people to knowledge of truth.

vihara A Buddhist temple or monastery.

Wicca Also called 'the Old Religion', 'witchcraft' or simply 'the Craft', this practice takes many forms, some involving esoteric rituals, others more concerned with alternative ways of healing.

yoga Bodily and mental exercises, breathing and postures that increase health and spiritual awareness.

yogic flying The practice of bouncing (usually about half a metre) which begins with meditation in a cross-legged position; believed by its adherents to convey health benefits.

Zoroastrianism The strongly ethical religion of ancient Persia, founded by Zoroaster/Zarathushtra, possibly related to the Vedic religion (*see* Parsi, Vedas).